KU-038-882

ASSESSING PHYSICALLY DISABLED PEOPLE AT HOME

FORTHCOMING TITLES

Occupational Therapy for the Brain-Injured Adult
Jo Clark-Wilson and Gordon Muir Giles

Multiple Sclerosis
Approaches to management
Lorraine De Souza

Modern Electrotherapy
Mary Dyson and Christopher Hayne

Autism
A multidisciplinary approach
Edited by Kathryn Ellis

Physiotherapy in Respiratory and Intensive Care
Alexandra Hough

Community Occupational Therapy with Mentally Handicapped People
Debbie Isaac

Understanding Dysphasia
Lesley Jordan and Rita Twiston Davies

Management in Occupational Therapy
Zielfa B. Maslin

Keyboard, Graphic and Handwriting Skills
Helping people with motor disabilities
Dorothy E. Penso

Dysarthria
Theory and therapy
Sandra J. Robertson

Speech and Language Problems in Children
Dilys A. Treharne

THERAPY IN PRACTICE SERIES

Edited by Jo Campling

This series of books is aimed at 'therapists' concerned with rehabilitation in a very broad sense. The intended audience particularly includes occupational therapists, physiotherapists and speech therapists, but many titles will also be of interest to nurses, psychologists, medical staff, social workers, teachers or volunteer workers. Some volumes will be interdisciplinary, others aimed at one particular profession. All titles will be comprehensive but concise, and practical but with due reference to relevant theory and evidence. They are not research monographs but focus on professional practice, and will be of value to both students and qualified personnel.

Assessing Physically Disabled People At Home

KATHLEEN MACZKA

Occupational Therapist and Day Hospital Manager,
Bethnal Green Hospital, London

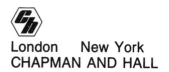

London   New York
CHAPMAN AND HALL

First published in 1990 by
Chapman and Hall Ltd
11 New Fetter Lane, London EC4P 4EE

Published in the USA by
Chapman and Hall
29 West 35th Street, New York, NY 10001

© 1990 Kathleen Maczka

Typeset in 10/12 Times by
Mayhew Typesetting, Bristol
Printed in Great Britain by
St. Edmundsbury Press, Bury St. Edmunds, Suffolk

ISBN 0 412 32480 6

This paperback edition is sold subject to the condition
that it shall not, by way of trade or otherwise, be
lent, resold, hired out, or otherwise circulated without
the publisher's prior consent in any form of binding
or cover other than that in which it is published and
without a similar condition including this condition
being imposed on the subsequent purchaser.

All rights reserved. No part of this book may be
reprinted or reproduced, or utilized in any form or by
any electronic, mechanical or other means, now known
or hereafter invented, including photocopying and
recording, or in any information storage and retrieval
system, without permission in writing from the
publisher.

British Library Cataloguing in Publication Data

Maczka, Kathleen
  Assessing physically disabled people at home. –
  (Therapy in practice; 12)
  1. Physically handicapped persons. Rehabilitation
  I. Title II. Series
  362.4'048
  ISBN 0 412 32480 6

Contents

Preface

In the current era of cost awareness and the pressure to free hospital beds as rapidly as possible, coupled with the move towards community care, there is increasing emphasis on returning and maintaining disabled people in the community. Often, many health and welfare workers are involved in this process. Occupational therapists however have a particular role to play. Their training is such that they are able to assess and treat the physical, psychological and social aspects of a disabling condition. This enables them to help disabled people to achieve their maximum ability in the environment in which they live. Whether the occupational therapist is hospital or community based, employed by the health or social service department, her caseload is often vast. The occupational therapist may specialize in a particular age group or disability, but it is more likely that she will have to work with a wide age range from the very young to the very old. Assessment of needs and the subsequent provision of equipment and adaptations is the greater part of the OT's job. Other aspects include counselling the disabled person and his family and planning future intervention must often, however reluctantly, be given a low priority. In spite of staff shotages occupational therapists are frequently called on to provide the client and other groups of workers with advice and information on all aspects of living with any disability.

This publication is an introduction to assessing disabled people in their homes. It is aimed particularly at students of occupational therapy, those who have recently qualified as occupational therapists and those who are returning to work after a period of absence. It includes details of the home visit. This is carried out with a disabled person prior to his discharge from hospital in order to assess practical needs and to organize services before discharge. The assessment of those already living in the community is also described.

Throughout the text the occupational therapist is referred to as 'she' and the patient/client as 'he'. References and suggestions for further reading are given at the end of each chapter.

Special thanks goes to Lisle Grassmeder who typed the original script.

1

The multi-disciplinary team in
the community

A disabling condition can have a profound effect on an individual and his family whether the condition occurs suddenly as the result of an accident, whether its onset is insidious, the result of old age, or at birth. Weller and Miller (1977) identified a four-stage process by which people newly disabled with paraplegia come to terms with disability. The way people react to disability varies greatly, but the following are common:

1. *Shock*. This is the immediate reaction. There may be weeping, hysteria and hallucinations
2. *Denial*. Refusal to accept that a complete recovery will not take place
3. *Anger*. Often directed towards physically active people nearby. They are a constant reminder of what has been lost
4. *Depression*. This is described as a realistic and appropriate response to a condition of severe and permanent disability. It is a necessary stage of adjustment if rehabilitation and integration are to be achieved

Fanshawe (1988) states that the effects of permanent disability are present throughout the day and night and will have a bearing on all activities. As a result, the people involved may need to re-think their lives and learn a new set of techniques for carrying out daily living skills as well as be aware of relevant benefits and legislation. In some instances they may need to change their employment and leisure pursuits. Relationships with other people may even need to be adjusted.

Albrecht (1981) state that many disabilities are the result of social conditions such as low income, social isolation and architectural barriers. Whilst occupational therapists cannot completely change the effects of a hostile environment, they do have a valuable role to play in working with people who have difficulty or who cannot manage their own care independently. Curry and March (1988) suggest that the occupational therapist's main aims are to assess a disabled person's difficulties in various daily activities, to encourage maximum return of function and to provide equipment where appropriate to assist this. Brechin and Liddiard (1981) write that occupational therapists can not only guide people in choosing the most suitable equipment for their needs, but can also train them and their carers in its use. For some people however, learning a new technique for carrying out an activity is of greater help. The occupational therapist therefore requires a knowledge of the range of available alternatives combined with an awareness of a disabled person's functional requirements at the present time and in the foreseeable future.

Whether employed by the health or social service department, the occupational therapist works within a legal and statutory framework. In many instances she also works under great pressure with limited resources, many demands on her time and rarely able to offer long-term intervention. Oliver (1983) argues that planned intervention is economically justifiable. It can have a preventive role and alleviate the need for more costly intervention later. Family and social breakdown could be prevented from occurring if there was consistent, planned support.

Occupational therapists are few in number and often work alone, but they are still part of a team of workers whose aim is to provide a service to disabled people. Professions overlap to a certain extent, but each worker has, by the nature of her training, particular skills and interests. Occupational therapists do need to be aware of the ability of other team members, not only on a broad basis, but as far as possible, on an individual basis also. Similarly, other professions need to be made aware of the role and scope of the work of occupational therapists. Liaison between workers is essential therefore if misunderstanding of roles or a duplication of effort is to be avoided.

The concept of 'key worker' is used in many departments. The key worker can be any member of the team depending on the need of the client. The person taking this role is responsible for co-ordinating the help given to the client and to provide continuity of care. Workers with specialist knowledge and expertise may be called on to undertake specific tasks. The following are brief descriptions of some of the professions who work with disabled people. The range of their work could vary between areas depending on local agreements.

Bathing attendants

Bathing attendants are employed by the health authority and referral is made usually through the district nursing service. Bathing attendants are auxiliary nurses whose role is to wash the client either in the bath or shower or to give a bed-bath. They tend to work mainly with elderly or severely handicapped people who can no longer manage to wash themselves independently. Bathing attendants should be familiar with the use of various bathing equipment and may request the installation of equipment by the occupational therapist. Some authorities may not employ bathing attendants, in which case bathing is normally carried out by the district nurse.

Chiropodists

Chiropodists are responsible for care of the feet. They deal with corns, callosities, malformed toe-nails, foot deformities, and infections not requiring surgery. In addition, chiropodists will give advice on the care of the feet and the prevention of foot deformities. Some chiropodists work in private practice whilst others are employed by the health service. Treatment can be carried out in clinics within hospitals or in health centres. Some chiropodists provide a domiciliary service or may carry out sessions in residential homes and day centres for the elderly or handicapped. In some areas, more especially rural areas, there are mobile chiropody clinics. Care of the feet, particularly cutting toe-nails is a problem faced by many disabled people due to their inability to reach the feet, poor co-ordination or poor hand function which means they are unable to handle scissors or nail cutters. As the demand for chiropody is usually far greater than the number of chiropodists available, there is normally a waiting list for treatment.

Referrals to the chiropodist may have to be made through the GP.

Community physiotherapists

Traditionally, physiotherapists carry out treatment in hospitals, but there is now a move towards treating people in their own homes. The treatment given is similar to that carried out in hospitals, namely, balance, mobility, muscle strength, joint mobility and chest care. Where appropriate, carers are involved in treatment so that it can be continued when the physiotherapist is not present. Receiving physiotherapy at home eliminates the frustration of waiting for hospital transport and is particularly helpful for those clients who experience discomfort in travelling.

Physiotherapists are for the most part employed by the health service and referrals are usually made through the GP. However, it is also possible to employ someone from private practice to administer treatment.

Dietitians

Dietitians usually work within the health service and may be hospital or community based. They are concerned with all aspects of diet. This might include teaching people to manage their own dietary treatment such as those suffering from bowel disorders, diabetes or kidney disease, and providing support and follow-up to individuals and their families. In research and investigation units, dietitians can help to diagnose some disorders by providing accurately-measured diets. Furthermore, they play a preventive role through nutrition education.

District nurses

As an alternative to hospital admission, routine medical care such as dressing wounds and ulcers, the removal of sutures, giving injections and checking medication, may be carried out in a person's home by the district nurse. Often she is required to bath people and help them to get up in the morning. District nurses may also be responsible for providing more specialist care for those who, for example, have under gone a mastectomy or who have asthma, or for people who are incontinent. Frequency of visiting will depend partly on the severity of the condition suffered by the client and the district nurse's pressure of work. Health authorities are responsible for employing district nurses who usually operate from health centres or from doctors' surgeries.

General practitioners (GPs)

GPs are responsible for making an accurate diagnosis, for providing appropriate treatment and where necessary for arranging for hospital referrals. In addition they are responsible for the long-term care and management of their patients.

GPs need to have a wide understanding of the facilities provided through the range of voluntary and statutory services if they are to be effective in steering their patients towards the services most appropriate to their needs. Although the training of GPs now tends to emphasize their role as a co-ordinator of services, it is a common complaint amongst therapists that some GPs know little – if anything – about rehabilitation. It is useful therefore if occupational therapists inform GPs of visits to be carried out to their patients and send copies of reports giving details of the outcome of visits.

Health visitors

Health visitors are qualified nurses who have taken additional training for their job. Their role is mainly a preventive and advisory one. Although health visitors are trained to work with all age groups, because they are few in number, the greatest bulk of their work tends to be in maternal and child health.

In some areas they may visit a person who has been discharged from hospital in order to see how they are coping since their return home.

Most health visitors are employed by the health authority and they are based in health centres, clinics or doctors' surgeries.

Educational authorities sometimes employ health visitors to work in the school health service. Occasionally the therapist may have contact with a health visitor working solely with elderly people.

Home helps

The home help service is operated by the social services department. If a disabled or elderly person is referred to the home help service, an assessment of his need is first carried out by the home help organizer. As with so many services there are local variations, but usually the home help's main duties are cleaning and shopping and in some instances they will cook simple meals and be responsible for laundry.

Not all employing authorities will allow home helps to carry out activities above floor level – such as window cleaning, changing curtains and cleaning high cupboards – because of their insurance implications.

Visits vary between an hour or two a week, to several hours each weekday. Home help outside these hours or at weekends is rare. In some areas users of the service may be asked to pay towards the cost of the home helps. In other areas it is unlikely that a person would qualify for the service if there are non-disabled members in their households.

Meals on wheels

Hot midday meals delivered to a person's home are usually provided by voluntary organizations such as the Women's Royal Voluntary Service (WRVS) or the British Red Cross Society (BRCS). Local authorities however usually give financial assistance, premises from which to operate and the loan of transport, equipment and staff.

Special diets such as those suitable for a person suffering from diabetes can usually be requested. In some areas meals on wheels can be provided seven days a week, in others meals are provided Monday to Friday only, but extra meals to cover the weekend can be delivered on Friday and which require to be heated up. Some authorities however will only provide meals on a weekday basis and individuals will have to make their own arrangements at weekends and over public holidays. There is a minimum cost for the meal.

If there is a high concentration of an ethnic group in a particular area then specialist meals may be provided by other voluntary organizations. Kosher meals may for example be provided for Jewish people.

Social workers

Whether based in hospitals or in social service departments, social workers are employed by the local authority. In addition, certain voluntary organizations also employ their own social workers. The training of social workers is generic (all social workers are trained to deal with any social work problem) but some specialize in certain groups of clients such as children, disadvantaged families, homeless people, the elderly or sensorily handicapped people. Social workers have wide-ranging responsibilities including legal and financial problems as well as personal and social difficulties.

Social work assistants

Social work assistants are unqualified social workers who work under the supervision of their qualified counterparts.

Speech therapists

Speech therapists are employed by the health service (in which case they offer treatment in hospitals, clinics, health centres and day centres), or by local education authorities (in which case they offer a service to schoolchildren). Speech therapists work with people with impaired speech or loss of speech. They are able to provide equipment for speech replacement which ranges from simple communication charts to more sophisticated speech aids such as a microcomputer. Speech therapists will also give advice on eating and swallowing problems.

Twilight nurses

Twilight nurses are usually auxiliary nurses whose job it is to put elderly or disabled people to bed each night.

Although the service is a valuable one, it is impossible to tailor it to suit individual preferences. Thus, some people go to bed earlier than they would prefer and others later. The occupational therapist may be asked to instruct twilight nurses in the use of hoists and other lifting aids or techniques. In addition, it may be necessary to help a person to re-organize his home in order to accommodate going to bed early. The therapist can help by arranging a bedpan or urinal to be provided, helping to set up a television remote control, an over-bed table to accommodate reading material and lighting within reach of the bed.

REFERENCES AND FURTHER READING

Albrecht, G. (ed.) (1981) *Cross National Rehabilitation Policies: A Social Perspective.* Sage, (Beverly Hills).

Brechin, A. and Liddiard, P. (1981) *Look at it this Way – New Perspectives in Rehabilitation*. Hodder and Stoughton in association with the Open University Press.

Curry, R. and March, H. (1988) In *Rehabilitation of the Physically Disabled Adult*, C.J. Goodwill and M.A. Chamberlain (eds). Croom Helm, Beckenham.

Department of Health (1988) *Discharge of Patients from Hospital Health*. Circular HC(89)5. Department of Health, Health Services Division 2, Room A426, Alexander Fleming House, Elephant and Castle, London SE1 6BY.

Department of Health (1988) *The Development of Services for People with Physical or Sensory Disabilities*. November 1988, HN(88)26 DHSS.

Fanshawe, E. (1988) In *Rehabilitation of the Physically Disabled Adult*, C.J. Goodwill and M.A. Chamberlain (eds). Croom Helm, Beckenham.

Goodworth, M.D. (1974) *An Examination of the Role of Occupational Therapists Outside Hospital*. Canterbury Health Services Research Unit, University of Kent.

Hunter, D.J. and Judge, K. (1988) *Griffiths and Community Care. Meeting the Challenge*. King's Fund Institute, London.

Oliver, M. (1983) *Social Work with Disabled People*. MacMillan, London.

Weller, D.J. and Miller, P.M. (1977) Emotional reactions to patient, family and staff in acute care period of spinal cord injury. Part 2. *Social Work in Health Care*, **3**, pp. 7–17.

2

Sources of referral and preparation for the visit

Sources of referral are as diverse as the client groups served. If an occupational therapist is working in a hospital, referrals are usually made by medical staff. A home assessment may not have been specifically requested on referral of the patient to occupational therapy, but if during the course of assessment it is felt that a visit to the patient's home is necessary, a referral may not be required. If the occupational therapist is employed in the community however, medical personnel are just one of the many sources of referral.

Referrals may come from any of the professionals already mentioned, from the disabled person himself, from a member of the family, a friend or neighbour. Referrals may be made in person, over the telephone or in writing and are not always taken directly by the therapist.

Some referrals tend to be vague with no indication of the client's need, whilst others are explicit with the need clearly stated. If details are jotted down on flimsy pieces of paper and left casually on a desk they are likely to be lost. The use of a referral form is therefore essential by all those staff who request the service or receive requests for service either over the telephone or in person.

Referral forms must be available in the building from which the therapist works. Good practice will dictate their use by relevant departments or offices like local hospital occupational therapy and physiotherapy departments, district nurse offices, GP surgeries, the home help and meals on wheels' office, specialist sections such as those dealing with visually handicapped people, local schools with responsibility for handicapped children and offices of voluntary organisations such as the Citizens' Advice Bureau. Use of a standard form will enable much information to be gained about the potential client and the problems he is experiencing. Prepared with this basic information, the therapist is able to make some decision about the degree of urgency of the visit. More importantly, when the visit does take place, the therapist can go along prepared, as far as it is possible, to tackle the problems.

The referral form must include the following:

- Name
- Address
- Telephone number
- Date of birth
- Next of kin
- GP
- Relevant medical history including hospital, school or centre, if any, attended
- Summary of present problems and reason for requesting the visit
- Days suitable for visit, a.m./p.m.
- Method of access
- Person making referral (name and contact number)
- Person taking referral
- Date taken
- Date received

Because there is usually a waiting list for visits it is good practice to have a simple form of acknowledgement to send to the person making the referral. For example, a tear-off slip at the bottom of the referral form or a separate pre-printed postcard.

If the client is already known to the department, several requests for service may have recently been made. It is important to locate the existing file or case notes, establish this information, and give the referral a *priority coding*.

Priority coding varies between authorities. What is assessed in one authority as an essential service may be viewed in another as only desirable. So much depends upon availability of resources, of staffing, the size of the case load, the waiting list for visits and financial restrictions.

If the client is not known then a new file must be opened as soon as his details have been noted.

A joint visit by the hospital and local authority occupational therapists is particularly helpful if there is a possibility that the patient may require specialized equipment or adaptations, or if a complex situation is envisaged.

The social service occupational therapist can give advice on available facilities and the level of funding available. Because of her daily experience she may have a greater understanding of environmental features and will be able to discuss the suitability of equipment for installation. In these instances, joint visits are an efficient use of staff time. They provide a continuity of care as patients usually become the responsibility of social service occupational therapists when discharged from hospital. A joint visit can also prevent misunderstanding between therapists on available resources. Thus, clients are not promised that which is not available.

PREPARATION FOR THE VISIT

Inevitably there are similarities between home assessments carried out by therapists working from hospital and those employed by social service departments. There are some differences in the preparation for the visit however, and a checklist may be helpful so that time, which is always at a premium, is not wasted.

Hospital-based therapists

If the assessment is to be carried out by a hospital-based therapist, the patient is either taken home for assessment and brought back to hospital, or it may be a discharge visit where the patient remains at home if he is able to cope satisfactorily. An assessment of the patient's ability to carry out daily living activities must be carried out in advance of the visit. This is essential so that problems can be highlighted and specific emphasis can be given to those activities during the visit. If during the course of assessment certain items of equipment have proven helpful to the patient when carrying out activities, then arrangements should be made to take them to the patient's home so that they can be tried out *in situ* and their suitability assessed. In some instances this may involve collecting the equipment from the social service department in advance.

Inform staff

Relevant hospital staff must be informed of the visit in advance. Nursing staff particularly will need to be reminded the day before so that meals can be cancelled and to avoid other appointments being made.

11

Clothing

Check that the patient has suitable outdoor clothing to wear for the visit. The patient should not be taken home in his night-clothes. It can be degrading to travel in this way even if it is by private car or ambulance. It can be even more humiliating to have to walk from the road to the front door dressed only in night clothes. Catheter bags, if worn, should be concealed.

Transport

There will be local arrangements about ordering transport such as how long in advance of the visit it needs to be arranged. The type of transport required should be established. Is the patient able to transfer to and from a standard two-door or four-door saloon car, or is a vehicle with a tail lift required? If extra equipment such as walking aids, wheelchair, commode, bathing equipment and so on is required, then a more spacious vehicle will be needed. Similarly, if several members of staff are to accompany the patient, then there must be sufficient room in the vehicle to accommodate them. If transport is required for the return journey this must be stated. Parking facilities need to be clarified especially if the dwelling is in an urban area.

Inform carers

Involved relatives and neighbours, professional and non-professional, need to be informed in advance of the visit. A convenient date and time must be organized if they are to be present during the visit. Information about access to the dwelling should be checked in advance with the patient and other family members. If there are stairs there is little point in arranging the visit for a patient unable to climb stairs. If there is a lift and the patient uses a wheelchair, check that the lift is large enough to accommodate the wheelchair. Relatives or carers may be able to check dimensions.

If the patient lives in a rural dwelling it is important to find out in advance about the state of the ground. It may be uneven, muddy or there may be obstacles such as cattle grids to overcome.

The availability of the door key and the address should be checked before leaving for the visit.

Other family members should be asked to keep domestic pets, especially dogs and cats under control until the patient is indoors and safely seated. Animals become excited especially if they have not seen a person for a period of time. They may jump at the patient and causing him to lose his balance and fall.

If young children are part of the household, ask for toys to be cleared from the floor in advance. Poor mobility and balance or sight can cause the patient to stumble over small items.

Items to take

If the patient is expected to prepare a meal or hot drink during his visit then ingredients must be either taken along or prepared by other members of the household who need to be instructed. If the patient lives alone and has been in hospital for a long period, gas, electricity and water connections must be checked. If the cooking facilities and heating are gas powered, a box of matches should be taken along also. Medication, protection for incontinence and lavatory paper may need to be taken.

Timing of the visit

Thought should be given to the timing of the visit especially if the patient is taking medication. He may, for example, be drowsy at certain times of the day as an after-effect of the medication. If the patient suffers from a condition such as rheumatoid arthritis, he may have stiff joints in the morning, but be tired by the afternoon. However, the visit must be realistic and reflect the patient's ability to cope at home including coping with pain, restriction in movement or drowsiness.

Home-assessment kit

A tape-measure is invariably required and should be taken on the visit. Avoid cloth measures as these have a tendency to stretch. A metal, self-winding measure is best with imperial and metric measurements displayed clearly. In addition, paper, assessment forms, pens and pencils should not be forgotten. A small home-assessment kit may be useful to have and this can be taken with the therapist on a visit.

Community-based therapists

If the therapist is community based and plans to visit a client at home it is useful to carry out the following preparations before visiting.

If possible, make an appointment with the client. If the client has a telephone then contact can be made in this way in order to establish a suitable time and date to visit, as the client may work, attend a day centre, have a hospital appointment or go to school. In addition, other family members or carers may be required to be present and the timing of the visit will need to be convenient for them also. Having made contact it is worth checking the address and available parking facilities if going by car. If telephone contact is not possible and there is time then an appointment card should be sent. Some departments have ready-printed cards which only require the date and time of the visit to be filled in and the name of the therapist to be expected.

Sometimes visits are made unannounced, but there is always the risk that no one will be at home. As there is often a fear of vandalism or bogus callers, disabled and elderly people may be fearful of allowing an unannounced stranger into their home.

If the referral identifies specific problems, then it is useful to take along a range of equipment which might help to relieve these. This could save the therapist making a return visit immediately, although a follow-up visit will inevitably be required.

It may be necessary to contact the client's GP to gain more details of his medical condition. Some GP's may ask for the client's permission before releasing information. Therapists should liaise with other staff involved with the client in order to gain relevant information about the client in advance to the visit.

A home-assessment kit similar to that suggested above should be taken on the visit.

3

Interviewing and assessing

When a therapist first visits a disabled person at home, only limited details of that person may be available. There may be no specific diagnosis other than, for example, stiff knees, rheumatism or that he is experiencing some problem in carrying out a particular activity, or alternatively, that the person caring for him is having a problem in doing so.

The objective of the first visit is to gain information in order to clarify the problem and to determine its nature and extent, thereby establishing:

- what he is able to do for himself
- what he would like to be able to do
- what he needs to be able to do
- what is required to enable him to carry out these activities for the present and in the future
- what other agencies are already involved

Once an informed starting point has been established then ways of solving the problem may be implemented.

It is obviously essential that the person experiencing the difficulty should be present at the visit, as should carers, so that first-hand information can be obtained and that services can be matched to individual needs and wants.

People's expectations of the visit will vary greatly. Some people may have never been visited by an occupational therapist or indeed anyone from the health service or social services department before. If they have not been instrumental in requesting a visit, perhaps the referral has been made by another agency such as the GP or district nurse, they may be puzzled about why it is to take place and what exactly it will entail. Generally, occupational therapy is still a little-known profession and some people may have never heard of it before or may believe it is concerned in some way with work.

Because of this uncertainty regarding the nature of the visit, feelings of anxiety on the part of the client may not be uncommon. He may feel that his lifestyle is going to be scrutinized or criticized and if he has rarely or never sought help before, he may be worried that he is giving the impression of being a scrounger. Alternatively, there may be feelings of scepticism if several people have visited previously. Perhaps the same person has never visited twice. There may have been promises of help which were never fulfilled, items delivered, but no one came back to check if these were correct or suitable for the individual concerned. As the problem may have never been solved then it is hardly surprising if in this instance the therapist is greeted with scepticism or indeed anger when the client is asked to relate the history of his problem yet again. Equally, the therapist may have preconceived ideas. There may have been reports from other workers involved, and clients may have been labelled as being difficult to deal with, demanding, unwilling to help themselves, and so on. The type of neighbourhood and condition of the dwelling may also influence the therapist in forming an opinion of what a person may be like even before meeting him. These are merely examples of situations which might occur. The therapist must try to be neutral and impartial and avoid making firm promises about taking a particular course of action if she is not wholly certain, for whatever reason, that it may not be possible.

Having arrived at the house, introductions are necessary: name, profession, place of work and a brief explanation regarding the reason for the visit. If an appointment card has been sent in advance then reference to this may clarify who the therapist is. Most authorities now issue employees with some form of identity card which can help in gaining access, especially as many people fear bogus callers. However, there are instances where the caller will be invited in even before she has had a chance to utter a word.

Interviews can be conducted in different ways and will vary on the degree of formality, but it should be possible at the close of the interview to establish the current level of functioning, what factors are causing difficulty, and if the diagnosis is known at this stage, it may be possible to provide a prediction as to the outcome.

In most cases the interviewer and interviewee will be complete strangers. Although time is always at a premium it is courteous to begin with 'small talk' as most people find difficulty in speaking immediately in an open and uninhibited manner about the personal and intimate aspects of their life.

Sometimes the interviewer may be offered a cup of tea. Although acceptance is an individual choice, it is often an excellent informal way of assessing a whole range of abilities: mobility, balance, use of a walking aid or manoeuvring a wheelchair. Upper-limb function may also be assessed: reach, grasp, co-ordination, safety and concentration can all be assessed. Any problems observed can be a starting point for conversation. It is impossible to compete with the loud volume of a television, radio or hi-fi system, and although the therapist is a visitor to the patient's home and must not forget this, it is in order to firmly but politely request that the volume be reduced so that the interview can be conducted without distraction.

A questionnaire or checklist is essential. It provides a useful reference point and gives structure to the interview. It is particularly helpful if words fail the interviewer or if questions may be forgotten. Some therapists feel that this method can inhibit the interviewee, but some reliable method of recording information must be adopted in order to prevent confusion and inaccuracy, especially if the visit is one of several carried out that day. Furthermore, if dependency can be briefly expressed in figures or words then a checklist makes possible comparison of a client's ability over a period. Assessment forms vary greatly. They are usually compiled on an *ad hoc* basis and may be lengthy. They have rarely been validated.

Goodwill and Chamberlain (1988) question whether several tests within each assessment are measuring the same dysfunction. They site the activities of daily living (ADL) section of the Stanford Health Assessment Questionnaire (Fries *et al.*, 1980). This originally included thirty such items. However, it was possible to reduce the questions to eight key areas with little loss of sensitivity. They go on to state that comparisons between different treatment methods or styles of management can be made more satisfactorily if well-established indices are used rather than a new or non-validated series of ADL tests.

One such test is the Katz Index of ADL Test (Katz *et al.*, 1963). This covers the assessment of bathing, dressing, going to the toilet, transferring from bed and chair, continence of urine and faeces, and feeding. Specific definitions of functional independence and depen-dence are given below the index. Independence is used to describe an activity carried out without supervision, direction or active personal assistance. If the person being assessed refuses to perform a function, he is considered as not performing the function although he may be physically able to do so.

An assessment which takes into account the home environment is the Spaulding Rehabilitation Hospital (SRH) Home Visit Evaluation Form (Rosenblatt *et al.*, 1986). Here the client's ability to negotiate the home environment is assessed. This includes his ability to perform specific tasks in the bathroom, kitchen, bedroom and living room, to manage housework and shopping, and to escape safely from the home. His ability to carry out the activity is recorded as unable, assisted, independent or not applicable. The therapist is also able to document her recommendations for changes in the home environment, any equipment used, the need for support services and any conclusions concerning safety. The SRH Home Visit Evaluation Form is used particularly with a discharge home visit.

Other standardized tests which the therapist might find helpful are the Barthel Scale (Mahoney and Barthel, 1965), the Frenchay Activities Index (Holbrook and Skilbeck, 1983), the Klein–Bell ADL Scale (Klein *et al.*, 1982) and the Northwick Park ADL Scale (Benjamin, 1976).

If the interviewee cites a problem then it is important to analyse the task and pin-point exactly what the problem is. For example, hair washing: is the inability or difficulty because the sink is too low, the person is unable to stand or bend over the sink, is unable to turn on the taps or dispense the shampoo, reach his hair, or has sufficient dexterity to apply shampoo and wash it? Impaired intellectual function, apathy or depression may account for poor performance. This must be noted.

The interviewee needs to be told clearly what is being asked of him. Care should be taken when using medical terminology and abbreviations. Some disabled people will be familiar with them and may use them freely during the interview to describe the cause and effects of the condition. Others will not. The way questions are posed, therefore, is important if a true picture of the situation is to emerge. Thus, trying to establish if someone needs to use the toilet frequently during the night can be done in several ways:

1. 'Do you experience a frequency of nocturnal micturition?'
2. 'Do you have trouble with your water works at night?'
3. 'How many times you need to pass water during the night?'

Sometimes people give what they feel are acceptable responses, which the interviewer wants to hear rather than a realistic account of the situation. Elderly people particularly may fear that they will have to give up their independence completely and even be taken into care if they admit that they are experiencing difficulty or are unable to complete an appropriate task independently. Carers may feel that the problems are a reflection of their inadequacies and inability to cope.

Withholding information does of course hamper the therapist's capacity to help, but people do have a right to secrecy. It may also reflect denial of a problem.

It is important that the interviewer does not assume in advance what the problems are. She should neither ask questions in a particular way which will lead to confirmation of her expectations (nor discount) any detail in what is being told to her.

Disabled people and their carers should be active participants and should make a major contribution to the interview. They should be given time to ask questions. The interviewer should, in turn, listen to what they have to say. This will lead to a more satisfactory understanding of the problem including the inappropriateness and inadequacies of the present situation.

The interviewer should establish what the person needs to do to get through the day, what his priorities are and what he would like to be able to do. Enquiries should be made not only about the problems encountered, but also the ways that have been found to solve them.

Apart from straightforward questions and answers, interviews may also be coupled with some test of practical ability. Thus, trying to establish a person's ability to transfer from a chair independently can be done in several ways:

1. By asking the question – 'Can you get out of your chair?'
2. By asking – 'Can you show me how you get out of your chair?'
3. If the client answered the door to the interviewee then he probably did get out of a chair to do so, but the activity may have been difficult. An indication of this may be the length of time it took to answer the door. Thus, the interviewer might ask – 'It seemed to take a little while for you to get to the door, is it a struggle to get out of your chair?' Or – 'I notice your chair is quite low, does that mean you have a struggle in getting out of it? It seemed to take a little while for you to answer the door'.

Some tasks such as dressing and undressing can be difficult to assess. Unless a good rapport has been established, people may feel it is inappropriate to be asked by a complete stranger to take their clothes off in the middle of the day.

However, it should be possible to establish some idea of independence through observation. For example, the state of their clothing, unfastened buttons or zips may indicate an area of difficulty and be a starting point for conversation.

Having completed the assessment there will probably be an overwhelming abundance of information which needs to be carefully analyzed in order to pin-point problems before proposing solutions. It usually takes time to carry out a full and complete assessment and the interviewer may have insufficient time to think of ways around every problem immediately.

Apart from daily living skills, other areas need to be considered, such as the disabled person and his family's acceptance of loss of function. This may well have a bearing on the amount of help, if any, a person will accept.

REFERENCES AND FURTHER READING

Bell, L. and Klemz, A. (1981) *Physical Handicap – a guide for the staff of social services departments and voluntary agencies* Woodhead-Faulkner, Cambridge.

Benjamin, J. (1976) The Northwick Park ADL Index. *British Journal of Occupational Therapy*, **39**, 301–7.

Brorsson, B. and Asberg, K. H. (1984) Katz Index of Independence in ADL. *Scandinavian Journal of Rehabilitation Medicine*, **16**, 125–32.

Eakin, P. (1989) Assessments of activities of daily living: a critical review. *British Journal of Occupational Therapy* January, 11–15.

Eakin, P. (1989) Problems with assessments of activities of daily living. *British Journal of Occupational Therapy*, February, 50–4.

Fries, J.F., Spitz, P., Kraines, R.G. and Holman, H.R. (1980) Measurement of patient outcome in arthritis. *Arthritis and Rheumatism*, **23**, 137–45.

Goodwill, C.J. and Chamberlain, M.A. (eds) (1988) *Rehabilitation of the Physically Disabled Adult*. Croom Helm, Beckenham.

Granger, C.V. and Gresham, G. (1984) *Functional Assessment in Rehabilitation Medicine*. Williams and Wilkins, Baltimore.

Holbrook, M. and Skilbeck, C.E. (1983) An activities index for use with stroke patients *Age Ageing*, **12**, 166–70.

Katz, S., Ford, A.B., Moskowitz, R.W., Jackson, B. and Jaffe, M.W. (1963) Studies of illness in the aged. The Index of ADL: a standardised measure of biological and psychological function. *Journal of the American Medical Association*, **185**, 914–19.

Klein, M. and Bell, B. (1982) Self-care skills: behavioural measurement with the Klein-Bell ADL scale. *Arch. Phys. Med. Rehabil.*, **63**, 335–38.

Mahoney, F.I. and Barthel, D.W. (1965) Functional evaluation: the Barthel Index. *Maryland State Medical Journal*, **14**, 61–5.

Rosenblatt, D.E. Campion, E.W. Mason, M. (1986) Rehabilitation home visits. *Journal of the American Geriatric Society*, **34** (6).

4

Working with people from ethnic groups

When the term 'ethnic group' or 'ethnic minority' is used in Britain, there is a tendency to apply it only to the Asian or black populations. There is also a tendency to apply very generalized information rigidly and assume that all ethnic groups behave in a similar manner and experience similar problems.

Instead, any culture either black or white which differs from that of the indigenous population should be included in the term. Britain has a long history of immigration and has received people from all over the world. White Europeans such as Cypriots, Italians, Southern Irish, East European and Jewish people all appear to have been assimilated fairly easily although many have retained aspects of their culture. There are similarities between their way of life and that of the indigenous population.

Immigrants from Africa, Asia and the Caribbean are often wrongly regarded as one group in spite of their very different languages, customs and backgrounds. Because their skin colour and facial appearance differs from that of the indigenous population they are more easily recognizable as immigrants than their white counterparts. Assumptions are often selectively and wrongly made about their perceptions and aspirations. Therapists should be sensitive to the needs of all individuals whatever their background. Disabling conditions, regardless of the client's country of origin can make demands at all levels of the health and social services and can also affect personal relationships. Country of origin does not indicate a greater, or lesser understanding of the range of statutory or voluntary organizations. Many people born in the United Kingdom experience considerable difficulty in obtaining information on services available to them, and in negotiating a path through the bureaucratic maze which often seems to surround their access to information.

Therapists may be oversensitive in their approach to clients of different ethnic backgrounds from their own. They may be worried about offending clients particularly when addressing them, communicating with them or discussing aspects of religion, dietary habits or their role within the family.

NAMES

Many ethnic groups organize their names in the same way that British people do. Hence, a title is given first, followed by a first name and then a surname. For example, Mrs Angelina Di Marcasi or Mr Josef Czarnecki. For a family from South-East Asia, however, this system does not apply as the members lack a common surname. Husbands, wives and their children may all have different names. This makes record-keeping difficult and it is not uncommon to hear of instances where treatment has been duplicated because there is more than one set of case notes.

In these instances it may be necessary to include the names of all family members in the records and state clearly their relationship to one another.

Therapists should not feel inhibited or embarrassed about asking families for guidance regarding names to use for individual family members and in which order they are placed. This is necessary to save much confusion in record-keeping and embarrassment when addressing people.

LANGUAGE AND COMMUNICATION

If possible it is helpful to establish the language spoken by the client before carrying out the first visit. This will save time and confusion as the client may be totally unaware of the therapist's role and the reason for the visit. The therapist may be fortunate enough to speak the same language as the client, but if not an interpreter will be required. Some authorities have access to interpreters specializing in a whole range of languages. Such a facility, if available, can be a tremendous help. Failing that, it may be necessary to use other members of the client's family to act as interpreter. If the client uses a relative or friend as interpreter, he may not wish that person to hear details of the intimate aspects of his life or bodily functions. If the therapist senses that such a problem exists it may be more sensitive to suggest the use of an independent interpreter.

If equipment is issued to help a person achieve independence in daily living, the therapist must feel confident that the client knows how to use it. Again this applies to all disabled people irrespective of their language. If written instructions are to be given, it is important to know which language to use and to avoid ambiguities.

DIETARY PRACTICES AND METHODS OF EATING

Not all ethnic groups use a knife and fork to eat their meals. Chinese people, for example, use chopsticks and for some foods will use a spoon, whilst some Asian people prefer to use their fingers to eat. If independent feeding is a problem then the therapist must know the habits practised and preferred by the client. Will it, for example, be possible to adapt chopsticks so that they can be used by a Chinese person who, as a result of a high-level spinal lesion, has very limited hand function, or might that person prefer to use a spoon fixed to a palmar cuff?

A person who is Muslim will only use their right hand for eating. It is unlikely that he would consider using his left hand as this is traditionally used for toiletting. If the right hand has been affected as the result of a stroke then alternative ways of independent feeding must be considered. However, the person may prefer to be fed by a helper rather than use his unaffected left hand.

An orthodox Jewish person will have two sets of cutlery in his kitchen for food preparation – one for use with meat and the other for use with dairy products. If he suffers from rheumatoid arthritis and cutlery needs to be adapted to promote his independence, then both sets of cutlery must be adapted so that independence is maintained.

There are so many variations and here again it must be established what the client's normal practice is and what he now finds to be acceptable. Dietary practice may also need to be discussed, particularly if the client is to be referred to another care agency such as a day centre or school, or if he is to receive meals on wheels.

RELIGIOUS BELIEFS

These are varied as is the seriousness with which they are adopted. Some religions have a bearing on diet and require certain foods to be excluded. At certain times of the year members of some religious groups are expected to fast or to eat food only at a specific time of day – Christians during Lent, for example, or muslims before the feast of Ramadan. If prayer is an important part of his life, a patient may wish to follow a particular ritual as far as his disability allows. For example, if praying at floor level is usual, a severely disabled person may use a hoist to lower himself to the floor. He may use the same hoist to assist with daily living activities such as transferring from bed, chair and toilet.

It is worth repeating that every client, regardless of his origin must be approached with sensitivity. Individual needs and preferences should be considered in the light of the service which can be provided. If the therapist is uncertain about particular customs, she must ask the client to explain them. In this way misunderstandings can be avoided.

REFERENCES AND FURTHER READING

Barnett, V. (1980) *A Jewish Family in Britain*. Pergamon Press.
Bridger, P. (1980) *A Hindu Family in Britain*. Pergamon Press.
Community Relations Commission. (1976) *Between Two Cultures*. Commission for Racial Equality, London.
Harrison, S. (1980) *A Muslim Family in Britain*. Pergamon Press.
Health and Social Service Journal (15.7.82). Asians in hospital – What's in a name?
Kings Fund Centre. (1982) *Ethnic Minorities and Health Care in London*. King's Fund Publications, London.
Levine, R. (ed.) (1984) The cultural aspects of home care delivery. *American Journal of Occupational Therapy*, **38** (11), 734–8.
Lobo, E.H. (1978) *Children of Immigrants in Britain – Their Health and Social Problems*. Hodder and Stoughton, Sevenoaks.
Owen, C.W. (1980) *A Sikh Family in Britain*. Pergamon Press.
Wilson, A. (1978) *Finding a Voice – Asian Women in Britain*. Virago, London.

5

Problem solving.
The provision of equipment

Disabling conditions affect people in many different ways both mentally and physically. A person's attitude towards disability and his relationships with family and friends will vary. The environment a person lives in will differ, as will his educational background and financial status. It is simply not possible therefore to impose one standard set of solutions per diagnosis following an assessment. All options need to be considered to ease the situation both immediately and in the future.

The therapist needs to have a full understanding of the nature and prognosis of the condition suffered by the client as this will have a direct bearing on the choice of solution. It will need to be established if the condition is short term or permanent. If permanent, then the degree of deterioration and subsequent loss of function should, as far as possible, be determined. It is always difficult to predict timespans, and liaison with the GP or hospital staff may be necessary to gain further information. A realistic prediction is essential so that solutions to the problems presented now will be adequate over a period of time, perhaps several months or years.

No attempt should be made to alter the home situation without a full and careful explanation to the individual and family involved. At all stages decision making must involve the client and his family. The therapist has no right to intervene or arrange for any course of action without the consent of those concerned. If there is reluctance on the client's part to accept solutions it may be that he is not fully aware or does not fully understand the implications. Often a person is reluctant to have changes made to his home. He may feel that the installation of equipment or adaptations reinforces disability and an inability to carry out activities. He may be worried about obtaining the permission of a landlord, or fear that the tenancy of the property or the rateable value of his home will be affected. Alternatively, a person may simply prefer to retain the *status quo* even though daily living is a struggle and some aspects of independence remain limited. Whatever the case, the final decision lies with the person concerned. The therapist can advise the client on the range of options open to him. It may even be possible to view and try out the options available. Full details to offset the cost incurred need to be discussed. If the solution is still unacceptable or a compromise cannot be reached, then the client has the final word and this must be respected. The therapist can then only help the person to be as independent as possible within the limitations posed by the present environment. It is important that the facts of the situation are carefully documented as they may need to be referred to at a later stage.

Some problems can be overcome quite simply by discussing and showing alternative ways of carrying out an activity which is difficult. Dressing, for example, poses a problem for some people with restricted movements. Easier methods of putting on garments, adaptations to fastenings or the choice of garment and type of fabric might make the task easier. The task of filling a kettle is difficult for someone who is unable to lift and carry heavy items. The provision of a mini-boiler which can be used to boil just one cup of water at a time is one way of solving this problem.

PROVIDING EQUIPMENT

The handicapping effects of disability can, in some instances, be lessened by providing equipment. Equipment may help a person to carry out, either independently or with less effort, an activity which they could not do before. In addition, selected equipment may make caring for a disabled person easier.

Numerous items are available on the market to do this. These vary from simple equipment such as a gadget to turn taps on and off, to more complicated equipment especially designed for disabled people. Examples of these may include aids to speech replacement, wheelchairs and hoists.

Most occupational therapy departments maintain a stock of commonly used items, but in most instances it is not practical, or funds are not available, to keep examples of more unusual, expensive or larger items.

Staff involved in the prescription and supply of equipment have

27

difficulty in keeping entirely up to date with new ideas and designs or modifications in design, or even with the vast array already available. It can also be difficult to be aware of the merits of one piece of equipment over another. However, if the equipment is to achieve its aim, then care must be given to its choice. If it is wrongly chosen or prescribed it will prove useless and in some cases hazardous, money will be wasted and the disabled person prevented from reaching his full potential.

Following assessment of need, the first step in problem solving must therefore be to seek information on just what is available. However, whilst looking for information about equipment, the following points should be borne in mind:

- What exactly is the problem which the equipment is meant to solve? This should have been established and defined during the assessment.
- What is the nature of the condition suffered by the client and how does this affect his ability to carry out daily living skills? This will include both his physical and mental state.
- In what environment will the equipment be used, is there sufficient space and will other members of the family be affected by it?
- How safe and easy to use is the equipment, is it reliable and good value for money?
- Does the product require installation and maintenance? If so, a system or person must be identified who will carry this out.

SOURCES OF INFORMATION (EQUIPMENT)

The following organizations can assist with information to help in the selection of equipment. They are listed in alphabetical order and addresses are given in Chapter 13.

Aids to Communication in Education Centre (ACE)

The ACE Centre aims to co-ordinate national developments in the use of micro-electronic equipment in education.

The Centre collates and disseminates information about micro-electronic equipment and provides a database about this for use by field workers. In addition, facilities are provided for those who wish to see and try out micro-electronic equipment.

British Database on Research into Aids for the Disabled (BARD)

The Handicapped Persons Research Unit at Newcastle Upon Tyne Polytechnic has a computerized register of non-manufactured equipment and related research projects. The register gives details of current designs, development projects, prototypes and one-off equipment. In addition there are details of evaluations, surveys and research in the use of equipment. BARD can answer specific enquiries.

British Telecom's Action for Disabled Customers (BTADC)

British Telecom issues a range of equipment to help disabled people overcome telephone communication problems. The BTADC programme has been established to keep people informed about what is available.

Disabled Living Foundation Information Service

The Disabled Living Foundation (DLF) collects, collates and disseminates information on equipment, adaptations, benefits and the range of services and facilities available to disabled people with the exception of purely medical matters. DLF Data, the computer-held information bank, is constantly updated. Information may be obtained in a number of ways as outlined below.

DLF Information Handbook

A complete set consists of 23 individual lists. These are updated yearly and revised lists, usually three or four, are issued bimonthly. No list should be more than twelve months old. Every list gives details of the most generally available equipment, brief descriptions and manufacturers' and major suppliers' names and addresses. In addition, relevant publications, other information sources and notes on supply are given. A bimonthly general information bulletin gives details of any changes, such as a manufacturer's address or an item being withdrawn from the market, before a new list is issued. Inclusion of particular items on lists does not indicate that they are recommended or tested by DLF. To get maximum benefit from the information therapists should ensure that the lists are kept up to date and altered where necessary. This will ensure that this comprehensive information about equipment is accurate.

Where therapists are not receiving lists, they should contact the DLF. This will establish whether the authority for which they work subscribes to the service, and if so, the name of the person or office in receipt of the information. Good communication is essential as, sadly, all too often lists are neatly filed away in offices where they are unused and inaccessible to those urgently requiring information.

The following lists are currently available:

Beds. Beds and accessories, mattresses, bedding, waterproof bed protection, enuresis alarms, self-lifting aids, bed and cantilever tables.

Pressure relief. Beds and cushions designed for pressure relief, sheepskins, inflatable and foam rings, advice notes.

Chairs. High seat, adjustable and mobile chairs, self-lift seats, raising blocks, footstools, sagbags and cushions.

Communication A. Reading and writing aids, page turners, tape recorders and radios, aids to speech and speech replacement, aids for deaf and hard of hearing people, visually handicapped people, useful organizations.

Communication B. Remote control apparatus, telephone aids, alarms and emergency call systems, and intercoms.

Eating and drinking aids. Cutlery, plates, heat-retaining items, trays, egg-cups, non-slip materials drinking aids and bibs.

Hoists and lifting equipment. Mobile, fixed and electric hoists, manual lifting aids, lifts and stair climbers, and car hoists.

Leisure activities. Social and youth clubs, holidays, sports, gardening, art, drama and music, hobbies and pastimes, reading and libraries, radio, TV, records and tape recorders.

Sports and physical recreation. Details of national organizations concerned with sports, physical education and recreation management, aids and adaptations, sports provision, publications, films and physical activities with mentally-handicapped people.

Personal Toilet. WCs, WC aids, commodes, bedpans, urinals and waste-disposal units.

Personal Care. Baths and bath accessories, shower equipment, hand basins, rails and personal care items, hand, hair and tooth care, cosmetic and menstruation aids and pill reminders.

Transport. Bicycles, tricycles, car controls and vehicle conversions, cars and motor cycles with special design features, lifting systems, accessories, hire of vehicles, tuition and insurance.

Walking aids. Walking frames, trolleys, crutches, walking sticks, stick seats and standing aids.

Manual wheelchairs. Self-propelling and push chairs, carrying chairs, ramps, wheelchair accessories and information on hire services.

Electric wheelchairs. Details of indoor and outdoor models, scooters, conversion units, accessories and hire services, advice and insurance.

Household equipment. Kitchen utensils, small cooking appliances, taps, trolleys, stools and steps, laundry and cleaning equipment, pick-up and reaching aids.

Household fittings. Gas and electric cookers and appliances, kitchen storage units, sinks, electric switches, flooring doors and door furniture, windows and curtains.

Notes on incontinence. Illustrated notes on the management of incontinence, the use of protective garments and other equipment; deodorants and neutralizers.

Clothing. Special clothing for wheelchair users, women who have undergone mastectomy, extra warm and weatherproof clothing, hosiery, sports and leisure wear, swimwear, foundation garments, underwear, nightwear and daywear, and notes on adaptations and reinforcements.

Footwear. Large, small and odd sizes, narrow and wide fittings and made-to-measure footwear, shoe adaptations, suitability for calipers and footwear accessories.

Children's aids – general. Eating and drinking aids, balance and exercise equipment, personal toilet, protective equipment, toys and play equipment.

Children's aids – mobility. Walking aids, pushchairs and wheelchairs, trolleys, go-karts and tricycles, slings, car seats and harnesses.

Children's aids – furniture. Chairs, desks, tables, floor-level furniture, support and standing aids, beds, play garden equipment.

Office furniture and equipment. Office chairs, desks, storage and filing units, guidance notes on office layout and choice of equipment (excluding computers, but a separate resource list is available).

A contents page and subject index accompany the Handbook.

If information cannot be found by consulting this then the DLF Enquiry Service should be used by writing or telephoning giving full details of the query.

The DLF has, in addition, four specialist advisory services which welcome enquiries. These are the music, visual handicap, clothing and footwear and incontinence advisory services.

The information service and the advisory services are staffed by qualified experienced professionals, usually occupational therapists and physiotherapists.

DLF has an excellent library on the non-medical aspects of disability and which supports the work of all its staff. The librarians can often help outside enquirers, by letter or phone. Therapists, researchers, and disabled people are welcome to visit, but because of space and staffing limitations, must make a prior appointment.

Northern Ireland Information Service for Disabled People

This is an information service similar to the DLF, but with particular reference to equipment which is available locally in Northern Ireland. Enquiries are dealt with by letter, telephone or visit. Subscribers to the service receive regularly-updated information sheets.

Scottish Council on Disability, Information Department

Again, this information service is similar to the DLF, but is relevant to Scotland. A pilot computer scheme using DLF data was set up in 1988. An enquiry service is available and a bimonthly newsletter on subscription.

Information lists covering the following topics are available and updated regularly:

- Beds
- Chairs
- Communication aids
- Eating and drinking aids
- Hoists and lifting equipment
- Leisure activities
- Sport and physical recreation
- Baths and showers
- Toilets and commodes
- Personal aids
- Transport – vehicles and accessories
- Transport – information and regulations
- Walking aids
- Wheelchairs
- Household equipment
- Household fitments
- Incontinence clothing and protection
- Notes on odour control and incontinence management
- Clothing for adults
- Voluntary organizations concerned with disabled people
- Children's aids and equipment
- Furniture for disabled children in schools
- Holidays
- Employment and training

DHSS Disability Equipment Assessment Programme

The Department of Health has set up an equipment evaluation programme in order to attempt some improvement in the provision of equipment for disabled people. The emphasis is on equipment for daily living as opposed to wheelchairs, orthotic devices or footwear. The method and results of the evaluations have been printed in the form of reports. There is an illustration and description of each item tested. One of the main advantages of the DHSS assessment programme is that not only professional workers but also disabled consumers are involved in the studies. The opinions expressed in the project reports are those of the consumer.

To date the following reports are available from DHSS, Health Publications Unit, No. 2 Site, Manchester Road, Heywood, Lancs. OL1D 2PZ:

- Assessment of adult cutlery
- Assessment of back rests for use in car seats
- Assessment of bath boards and bath seats
- Assessment of bath lifts
- Assessment of bathing aids for handicapped children (bath chairs, supports and inserts)
- Assessment of car handbrake adaptations
- Assessment of car mirrors
- Assessment of car seat belt adaptations
- Assessment of car steering wheel knobs
- Assessment of cooking utensils for rheumatoid arthritis patients (saucepans, cooking baskets and steamers)
- Assessment of feeding for handicapped children (spoons, beakers and handstraps)
- Assessment of furniture designed for handicapped children. Part I (corner seats, corner seat tables, chairs with detachable trays and ladder back chairs). Part II (adjustable tables, chairs without trays and standing aids)
- Assessment of high stools and chairs for use in the kitchen or at a high work bench by disabled people
- Assessment of irons and ironing boards
- Assessment of long handled reachers
- Assessment of manual bed aids
- Assessment of replacement car seats
- Assessment of self-rise chairs and cushions
- Assessment of sewing and knitting equipment
- Assessment of tables (specialised tables and work centres, small cantilever tables and bed tables/lap trays)
- Assessment of supplementary car mirrors
- Assessment of toilet aids for handicapped children
- Assessment of the use of lower limb dressing aids
- Assessment of woodwork tools

- Assessment of writing aids
- Community study of the performance of incontinence garments
- Comparative assessment of three types of moulded body support
- Easy chairs for the arthritic
- Food preparation aids for those with neurologican conditions – screw-top jar and bottle openers, can openers, vegetable peelers, stabilizers
- Food preparation aids for rheumatoid arthritis patients – screw-top jar and bottle openers, can openers, vegetable peelers, stabilizers
- Food preparation aids for rheumatoid arthritis patients. Part 2A (kitchen knives, scissors). Part 2B (food choppers, graters, food processors). Part 3 (whisks, hand-held blenders, electric mixers)
- Incontinence aids for handicapped children carried out in the Brent and Harrow Area Health Authority
- Office seating for the arthritic and low back pain patients
- Wheelchair cushions: Summary report.

Equipment for the disabled

Equipment for the Disabled (E for D) is a series of books covering most aspects of daily living. E for D differs from the comprehensive DLF information lists in that they cover fewer items of equipment and they are not updated as frequently. They are however illustrated and provide guidelines or points to consider when selecting specific items. Items ranging from specially designed to home self-made equipment are given. Most of the equipment shown in the publications has been used by disabled people and its use assessed by a therapist. The comments made on the equipment's suitability may be helpful to those who have to select from a range.

Because space is limited this may preclude the inclusion of several items of one type of equipment. Care is taken to ensure that the equipment shown is available at the time of publication and will remain so for at least another year. The books are revised on a rota system usually every five or six years.

Titles in the series are: *Communication Clothing and Dressing for Adults, Incontinence and Stoma Care, Home Management, Outdoor Transport, Wheelchairs, Leisure and Gardening, Disabled Mother, Personal Care, Housing and Furniture, Hoists and Lifts, Walking Aids, Disabled Child.*

TRYING OUT EQUIPMENT

After obtaining information and identifying equipment which it is felt might solve the problem, the next stage is to try the item out in order to ensure that it is satisfactory and is acceptable to the potential user.

It has already been mentioned that most departments will maintain a stock of equipment. If the item required is held in stock then it should be possible to take it directly to the client's home where it can be tried out and perhaps left for a trial period. A decision can then be made as to whether it meets the needs of the user.

Some equipment is not held in departments because it is too large, too expensive, or rarely needed. If this is the case ways must be found to obtain access to and try out equipment.

1. Local hospitals, day centres and residential homes may have the equipment in use. Often it will be possible to arrange to take the client along in order to view the equipment and try it out. Regular liaison with heads of departments, centres and homes is worthwhile in order to keep up to date with the equipment they are using and to receive comments from staff on the effectiveness of particular items.

2. A record should be kept of all equipment previously issued to clients. Some clients may agree to visits to their home by other potential users of the equipment. Before arranging for such a visit, it is vital that the therapist has the full agreement of all concerned. She must not assume that because she may have been instrumental in obtaining the equipment in the first place that she has an automatic right of entry or to use another person's home as a show-house.

3. Many firms are prepared to arrange for a demonstration in a client's home of a particular item they manufacture. Local representatives may already be known to the therapist. If not, then contact with the manufacturer's head office will establish if such arrangements can be made locally.

4. In recent years there has been a growth in the number of Disabled Living Centres not only throughout the United Kingdom, but also in overseas countries. The aim of the centres is to provide practical information by exhibiting a comprehensive range of aids and equipment. Disabled people may visit the centres either alone or accompanied by professionals, carers or family in order to try out a range of equipment. Every centre is different but they all

hold/display a representative cross-section of items available to assist all disabilities. Items on show should include beds, chairs, communication aids, aids to eating and drinking, hoists and lifting equipment, aids to personal hygiene, mobility aids, wheelchairs, household equipment, examples of clothing and footwear suitable for disabled people, children's aids and equipment. Examples of aids to employment and leisure activities may also be on display as well as equipment to help those who are hard of hearing or have poor vision. There may be photographic displays of suitable architectural features showing access to buildings or adaptations to property.

Equipment is not on sale at the centres, but descriptive leaflets and information on sources of supply and cost are available.

It is always advisable to make an appointment before visiting to ensure that the centre is open to visitors. (Some centres organize seminars and courses and may be closed to visitors on particular days.) Appointments are also necessary to ensure that the centre staff are available to demonstrate equipment and provide information.

Before arranging to visit a centre, its proximity to a client's home must be considered. If the distance is great and transport is difficult, then fatigue may be a problem. If the client is fatigued he may be unable to use the equipment on display to the best of his ability. Not all centres are able to provide facilities for refreshments and the centre may not be situated close to accessible cafeterias or restaurants.

If the visit is to be a lengthy one, it may be necessary to bring refreshments along, and, where appropriate, extra protection for those who are incontinent, perhaps even a change of clothing is essential.

The premises should be physically accessible to disabled people, but not all have car-parking facilities, so it is worthwhile checking this when making an appointment. The following Disabled Living Centres offer a fully comprehensive service:

Belfast	Disabled Living Centre, Prosthetic, Orthotic and Aids Service, Musgrave Park Hospital, Stockman's Lane, Belfast BT9 7JB
Birmingham	Disabled Living Centre, 260 Broad Street, Birmingham, West Midlands B1 2HF
Caerphilly	Resources (Aids and Equipment) Centre, Wales Council for the Disabled, Caerbragdy Industrial Estate, Bedwas Road, Caerphilly, Mid-Glamorgan CF8 3SL
Cardiff	The Demonstration Aids Centre, The Lodge,

	Rookwood Hospital, Llandaff, Cardiff, South Glamorgan
Dublin	National Rehabilitation Board, 25 Clyde Road, Dublin 4.
Edinburgh	Disabled Living Centre, Astley Ainslie Hospital, Grange Loan, Edinburgh EH9 2HL
Leeds	The William Merritt Disabled Living Centre, St Mary's Hospital, Greenhill Road, Leeds, West Yorkshire LS12 3QE
Leicester	TRAIDS (Trent Region Aids, Information and Demonstration Service), 76 Clarendon Park Road, Leicester LE2 3AD
Liverpool	Merseyside Centre for Independent Living Youens Way, East Prescott Road, Liverpool 14
London	Disabled Living Foundation, 380 – 384 Harrow Road, London W9 2HU
Manchester	Disabled Living Services, Disabled Living Centre, Redbank House, 4 St Chad's Street, Cheetham, Manchester M8 8QA
Newcastle upon Tyne	Newcastle Upon Tyne Council for the Disabled, The Dene Centre, Castles Farm Road, Newcastle Upon Tyne NE3 1PH
Nottingham	Nottingham Resource Centre for the Disabled, Lenton Business Centre, Lenton Boulevard, Nottingham G7 2BY
Sheffield	Sheffield Independent Living Centre, 108 The Moor, Sheffield S1 4DP
Southampton	Southampton Aid and Equipment Centre, Southampton General Hospital, Tremona Road, Southampton SO9 4XY
Stockport	Disabled Living Centre, Stockport Area Health Authority, St Thomas' Hospital, Shawheath, Stockport, Cheshire
Swindon	Swindon Centre for Disabled Living, The Hawthorn Centre, Cricklade Road, Swindon, Wilts. SN2 1AF.

There are in addition a number of centres which offer a limited service. Details can be obtained from The Disabled Living Centres Council, care of The Disabled Living Foundation.

Having considered all the options available, if the problem still remains unsolved consideration will have to be given to other possibilities.

Manufacturers will, in some instances, be willing to adapt their equipment to suit particular disabilities. Some may be willing to produce a one-off variation on the basic design. Slings for use with hoists are an example of such an item. Failing this, other options include the following:

The first option is approaching local educational institutes. Students of design, engineering, woodwork, or metal-work departments, for example, may be willing to provide creative solutions to daily living problems.

However, students and their lecturers will for the most part have very little or no knowledge of disabling conditions and the effect of these conditions on people. For this reason they will need to be given a very thorough brief and close liaison will be necessary throughout the project.

It is important that they are made aware of products already available so that a great deal of time and effort is not wasted re-inventing the wheel.

Before embarking on such a project, payment for the completed item will need to be discussed. An expenditure limit will need to be established. This should be made clear and agreed to by all parties involved and confirmed in writing.

The time-scale for completion will also need to be discussed and agreed. Usually students are unable to devote their whole time to a project. In addition, they normally work only in term time and not during holidays.

The second option is the Rehabilitation Engineering Movement Advisory Panels (REMAP). REMAP is a national organization with local autonomous panels throughout England, Scotland and Wales. The organization is made up of volunteers from many different backgrounds including carpenters, doctors, engineers, nurses, occupational therapists and physiotherapists.

Their aim is to design and produce adapted equipment for individual disabled people regardless of their disability – physical, psychological or sensory – provided the equipment is not already available on the market. They will however adapt commercially-available items.

Local panels meet regularly to review progress of existing projects, to receive new clients for discussion and to allocate work for design and action.

Referrals are accepted from any source. Most people referred are visited at home by members of the panel to discuss their problem *in situ* so that there is a total understanding of the need.

The equipment is tried out at all stages during its design and manufacture.

Individual disabled people supplied with equipment are rarely asked to pay for the item. This is because REMAPs members offer their skills without charge. In addition, they often use unwanted or discarded industrial materials. In some instances practical help is offered by private and government engineering workshops, apprentice schools, colleges of further education, polytechnics and other similar organizations. Social service departments do sometimes make grants for specific projects.

An index of items made is kept at the national headquarters. It is also possible to obtain details of local groups through them.

Widely differing equipment has been made including items for personal care, mobility, leisure, communication, education and medical equipment.

So far, it has been assumed that the therapist will be responsible for arranging for the provision of the equipment. However, some disabled people and their families may prefer to purchase their own equipment, but may ask the occupational therapist to guide them in choosing the item most suited to their needs.

There are manufacturers who offer a mail-order service or may have their own showrooms where sales can be made.

It is also possible to purchase some items through chemists and department stores, such as bathing and toiletting aids, aids to continence, eating and drinking, wheelchairs, high armchairs and kitchen items.

The therapist's role is again to provide information on what is available. This is an essential part of being able to help clients to select appropriately.

OBTAINING EQUIPMENT

Equipment may be provided to disabled people in several ways. In some instances, particularly with items which may serve the needs of disabled people for nursing care and for daily living, the supply of equipment may vary according to local arrangements between health authorities and local authority social service departments.

Disablement Services Authority (DSA)

Wheelchairs are provided by DSA which is part of the Department of Health. The range available covers the needs of users of all age groups from the very young to the very old, and includes non-powered wheelchairs (both occupant and attendant propelled), hand-propelled or pedal tricycles, electrically-powered occupant-controlled indoor chairs, and electrical attendant controlled outdoor chair. A maintenance and repair service, which is free of charge, is provided by DSA.

A whole range of accessories is available to wheelchair users including cushions to prevent pressure sores, moulded seat shapes, lifting seats and wheelchair narrowers.

Artificial limbs, wigs and artificial eyes are also available through DSA on the recommendation of a hospital consultant or hospital ophthalmologist.

Community Health Services

Equipment provided by health authorities is often referred to as nursing aids. Equipment is provided free and is usually available at the discretion of the GP, health visitor or district nurse. Examples of such items include ripple beds, commodes, urinals, bedpans, incontinence equipment and supplies, and in some instances, hoists.

Voluntary organizations such as the British Red Cross Society act as agents for health authorities in some regions and are responsible for the supply of equipment.

Department of Health (DH)

The DH will provide environmental controls for severely disabled people who are only capable of minimal movement. A referral is required by a GP or hospital consultant. In England referrals are made to regional or district health authorities. In Scotland they are made to the Scottish Home and Health Department, and in Wales to the Welsh Office. Applicants are assessed by specially appointed medical consultants to see whether they meet the criteria laid down for the supply of such equipment.

Hospital Appliance Service (NHS)

Items available on medical prescription include elastic stockings, stoma appliances, special footwear, supports, corsets and wigs. A charge may be made for some items. In addition, hearing aids are available as are aids for those with impaired sight, low vision aids including hand magnifiers. This equipment however is prescribed on free loan.

Local Education Authority (LEA)

School children and students with a disability who require equipment for educational purposes can obtain it through LEAs.

Special allowances may be paid to disabled students in higher education should they incur additional expenditure as a result of attending the course.

In Scotland, the Scottish Education Department is responsible for the assessment and payment of student grants.

Manpower Services Commission (MSC)

The MSC can provide grants of up to £6000 to employers if special equipment or adaptation to premises is required to help with employment for disabled people, including visually handicapped people. Severely disabled people who are unable to use public transport to get to work may claim assistance for alternative means of transportation if extra costs are incurred as a result.

Social Service Departments (local authority)

In spite of legislation which requires local authority social service departments to meet any disabled person's need for equipment which the department has accepted as necessary for safety, comfort and convenience, there are local variations on exactly what is available. The equipment available should include items for dressing, eating, food preparation, recreation, sitting, toileting, walking and washing.

However, the amount of money allocated for this equipment varies considerably. Where a person lives may determine the speed at which needs are met and exactly what is available to meet their needs.

Some equipment may be subject to a charge at the discretion of the authority concerned. When equipment is issued the client usually signs a loans agreement form stating that he will return the equipment when it is no longer required. Some social service departments may operate a policy of re-issuing returned equipment. This may not be practical or hygienic in some instances especially with aids for toiletting, bathing and personal care.

Value Added Tax (VAT) exemption

Some specialized equipment used by disabled people may be zero-rated of VAT. This exemption is extended to charities which serve disabled people. The relief covers the following items:

- Medical or surgical appliances designed solely for the relief of a severe injury or abnormality
- Chair lifts or stair lifts designed for use in connection with wheelchairs
- Commodes and toilet equipment
- Beds which are electrically or mechanically adjustable
- Hoists and lifting devices
- Motor vehicles designed or adapted to carry a disabled person in a wheelchair or on a stretcher.
- Clothing, footwear and wigs if they relieve a severe abnormality or injury or have been designed solely for the use of a disabled person
- Wheelchairs and invalid carriages
- Artificial respirators, oxygen concentrators, venal haemodialysis units
- Parts and accessories designed solely for the use of these items are also exempt of VAT
- Some goods are excluded from relief. These are contact lenses, dentures, hearing aids, (but not those which have been designed for the auditory training of deaf children) and spectacles
- In addition, relief is allowed on a number of services namely adapting, repairing or maintaining goods

Obtaining funds from charitable sources

If statutory authorities are unable to provide sufficient funds to cover the cost of equipment, then alternative methods of raising money must be considered. The individual and his family may be able to contribute an amount towards the cost depending on their financial situation.

If there is still insufficient money then charitable sources may be considered to meet the amount outstanding.

Raising money can be extremely time consuming. If an application is to be made on behalf of a client then it is important that it is made as clearly as possible. It should not be assumed that organizations will automatically understand the handicapping effects of disability on individuals.

Some charities may ask for an application form to be completed, but in other instances a letter will be required. Details to be included in the letter are:

- Name, address and date of birth of the person requiring help
- Details of the disability; date of onset, effects of disability, treatment required
- Social situation including occupation, past or present, if relevant
- Reasons for application for funds. It is important to state clearly why a specific item of equipment is required and exactly how it will help the disabled individual. Abbreviations should not be used when describing equipment as they may not be understood. It will need to be stated why the equipment is not available through the statutory authorities
- The exact amount of money required from charitable sources. The amount to be contributed by the individual or statutory sources needs to be stated
- Details of the applicant's financial situation; their income and expenditure will need to be included
- Other organizations which have been approached should be mentioned.

Publications which give details of grant-giving charities should be available for reference in public libraries. The following may make selection of the appropriate charity easier: *Directory of Grant-Making Trusts, Charities Digest* and *Guide to Grants for Individuals in Need.* The most relevant organizations should be approached first; for example, national organizations concerned with specific disabilities, the armed services or trade union welfare funds.

Local groups such as schools, colleges, pubs, social clubs, Rotary clubs, The Round Table and so on should be considered where appropriate.

FOLLOW UP

The importance of follow-up visits by therapists cannot be stressed enough. Studies carried out by the Institute of Ergonomics at Loughborough University have shown that at least 50% of items of equipment delivered to people's homes were not used.

Not only is this wasteful in terms of resources which are already scarce, but may lead to frustration and distress on the part of the client and his family who continue to struggle with daily living activities.

Reasons for non-use of equipment may be:

1. The equipment prescribed does not solve the problems created by the disabling condition.
2. The equipment is unsuitable for the environment in which it is to be used.
3. The equipment may lack durability and break down.
4. The user feels unsafe and insecure whilst using the equipment.
5. The equipment is not an acceptable solution to the problem of the individual concerned.
6. The client does not know how to use the equipment (e.g. if there was insufficient follow-up and instruction).

The aims of follow-up visits are:

1. To ensure that the item delivered is the correct one. Items may have been incorrectly addressed or confused with an order for another client.
2. To check that the item has been correctly installed and is functioning satisfactorily.
3. To instruct the user, his carers and family in the correct use of the equipment. The full range of use of the item should be covered no matter how obviously simple or straightforward it may seem to the therapist. It may, in addition, be necessary to leave written instructions.

The client should be able to perform all tasks which are necessary for the effective use of the product and feel safe and confident in doing so. Thus it is necessary:

1. To discuss the user's feelings and those of his family about the equipment and whether they feel it is acceptable in their home and as part of their life.

2. To ensure that the client is aware of who to contact should the equipment cease to function, or function incorrectly or ineffectively.
3. To check if the equipment is required any longer.

Although time is always at a premium and therapists usually have lengthy waiting lists of people requiring visits, follow-up visits should be repeated regularly. Even though they are time consuming, they are essential if the quality of service to disabled people is to be maintained. This is of particular importance if the client suffers from a condition which is likely to deteriorate.

Further visits are carried out:

1. To establish if there have been changes in the condition suffered by the client which means he is no longer able to use the equipment effectively.
2. To establish if the product is still functioning correctly.
3. To establish that the user and his family have not forgotten how to use the equipment.
4. To establish if the equipment is still acceptable to the client.

Once the therapist feels confident that the equipment is being used effectively, follow-up visits may be discontinued, but clients should be given a name and telephone number to contact should difficulties arise in the future.

REFERENCES AND FURTHER READING

Charities Digest (annual). Family Welfare Association, 501–505 Kingsland Road, London, E8 4AU.

Cooper, S. and Feeney, R.J. (1978). *Aids and Equipment for Disabled People – a Feasibility Study with the Setting Up of a Resource Group.* Institute for Consumer Ergonomics.

Coopers and Lybrand Associates Limited (1988). *Information Needs of Disabled People, their Carers and Services Provided.* Coopers and Lybrand, London.

Council of Europe Information Systems on Impaired, Disabled and Handicapped People (1982) Strasbourg, Council of Europe.

Darnbrough, A. and Kinrade, D. (1988) *Directory for Disabled People: A Handbook of Information and Opportunities for Disabled and Handicapped People*, 5th edn. Woodhead-Faulkner, Cambridge.

Directory of Grant-Making Trusts (annual). Charities Aid Foundation, 48 Pembury Road, Tonbridge Wells, Kent TN9 2JD.

Disabled Living Centres Council (1988) *Information Dissemination for Disabled People, their Carers and Service Providers. Conference Proceedings, 29 September 1988.* Disabled Living Centres Council, c/o Disabled Living Foundation, London.

Disabled Living Foundation Information Services Handbook. Annual update. DLF, London.

Directory of Grant-Making Trusts (annual). Charities Aid Foundation, 48 Pembury Road, Tonbridge Wells, Kent TN9 2JD.

Elwes, N.D.B. (1973) *Aids for the Handicapped: A Parents' Guide to the Supply and Use of Equipment for the Handicapped.* Spastics Society.

Feeney, R.J. and Galer, M. (1978) *Selecting aids for disabled people: General Guidelines for the Purchase and Provision of Products Designed for the Elderly and Disabled.* Institute for Consumer Ergonomics and National Corporation for the Care of Old People.

Guide to Grants for Individuals in Needs (1987). Directory of Social Change, Radius Works, Back Lane, London NW3 1HL.

Hale, G. (ed.) (1983) *The New Source Book for the Disabled.* Heinemann, (1976) London.

Hillingdon, London Borough of, *Domiciliary Services Evaluation.*

Part II. Five Types of Aid in Common Use. Social Services Research.

Information Services, a Review of Aids for People with Disabilities. (1984) RICA.

Keeble, U. (1984) *Provision of Aids and Adaptations for Hospital Patients Discharged into their own Home.* Kings Fund Centre.

Keeble, U. (1979) Aids and adaptations. Bedford Square Press.

Manning, M. (ed.) (1982) *Aids for the Disabled.* Community Care/IPC Business Press. (1982)

Millard, D. (1984) *Daily Living with a Handicapped Child.* Croom Helm, Beckenham.

Nicols, P. Haworth, R. and Hopkins, J. (1981) *Disabled – an Illustrated Manual of Help and Self Help.* David and Charles, Newton Abbot.

Ritchie, J. and Cook, J. (1981) *Information Services as Aids for Disabled People.* Social and Community Planning Research.

Ward, P.R., Numeiry, M.A. and Williams, P.O. (1979) *The Supply of Aids to Physically Handicapped People.* Institute of Biometry and Community Medicine. University of Exeter.

6

Housing adaptations

Apart from, or in addition to, the provision of equipment, a client's home may require alterations or adaptations to enhance his independence or to make caring for him easier. Alterations which are non-structural are usually referred to as minor adaptations. Normally the costs involved are relatively low and may be borne by the local authority. As the structure of the client's home is unchanged, an architect will not usually be involved. The requested work, for example, fixing a hand-rail beside the WC is usually carried out by a technician or may be contracted out if technicians are not employed by the local authority. In some instances, family members may be prepared to undertake the work themselves, but may need guidance regarding the purchase of suitable materials and the correct positioning of them.

If major adaptations are to be considered as a means of solving environmental problems, it will be essential for the occupational therapist to work closely with both the architect and the builder involved in the scheme. Such work might include widening or altering doorways, the installation of lifts, stair lifts or ceiling-mounted hoists, the provision of ramps, bathrooms and showers, or the building of an extension.

PAYMENT FOR ADAPTATIONS

Joint circular 59/78, the Department of the Environment *Adaptations of Housing for People who are Physically Handicapped* (HMSO, 1978) acknowledges that adaptations to housing for disabled people are important.

Under the Chronically sick and Disabled Persons Act 1970, social service departments have a responsibility for identifying, assessing and advising on the housing needs of individual disabled people, including the need for adaptation of their homes. In addition, they have a statutory duty under the Act to meet the need for equipment and adaptations in the home. This applies to a person with a permanent and substantial handicap of any kind. Usually people whose disability is clearly temporary are not included.

There are a number of different ways of obtaining finance to cover the cost of adaptations to the home. Whatever means is sought however, finance needs to be agreed before the work begins as usually grants are not given once the work is in progress. The ownership of the dwelling to be adapted will determine the type of financial help which can be sought.

Council tenants

Usually local authority housing departments will take responsibility for structural adaptations to their own property. Intermediate and improvement grants may also be applied for.

Housing association tenants

Individual housing associations may agree to finance adaptations through house renovation grants or housing association grants. Alternatively, tenants may apply for intermediate and improvement grants.

Owner occupiers

Intermediate and improvement grants can be applied for. The backing of the local authority social service department will normally be required.

Private tenants

The consent of the landlord is necessary before adaptations can be carried out. Intermediate and improvement grants can then be applied for either by the landlord or the tenant.

49

Improvement grants

The purpose of the grant is to pay for any structural work which is needed to make a dwelling suitable for the accommodation or employment of a disabled person where the existing dwelling is inadequate or unsuitable.

Improvement grants are discretionary, their allocation depends on an individual council's policy and resources. Improvement grants are usually not repayable, though a client must agree to occupy the adapted property for a period of five years.

Intermediate grants

Intermediate grants are mandatory, not discretionary. They are used to provide additional standard amenities where the existing ones are not readily accessible to the disabled occupant. The following are regarded as standard amenities:

- Indoor WC
- Fixed bath or shower with a hot and cold water supply
- Wash handbasin with a hot and cold water supply
- Sink with a hot and cold water supply

A grant will only be considered following the submission of a completed application form. This gives details of the estimated costs and plans of the proposed project. Once the work has been completed and inspected by the Environmental Health Officer (EHO), payment of the grant will be made. The amount of grant, improvement or intermediate, given in individual cases is based on the total cost of the approved work. This is referred to as the 'eligible expense' limit. Usually a grant of up to 75% of the total cost of the work is made, but in cases of financial hardship a 90% grant may be given.

If the applicant is unable to meet the remaining cost then there are several means of obtaining the outstanding amount:

1. Social service departments may cover the balance.
2. Social services or the housing department may offer a loan to cover the balance with the capital repayable on death or the sale of the house.
3. An application may be made to a bank or building society for a

loan or to extend an existing mortgage. (Interest payments on loans are eligible for tax relief.)

VAT exemption on house adaptations for disabled people

VAT is now charged on almost all alterations to buildings. However, some work related to housing adaptations for disabled people can be zero-rated. This includes:

1. The widening of doors and passages and the construction of ramps to allow a disabled person access to and manoeuvrability within the home.
2. The extension, alteration or provision of a bathroom, washroom or lavatory for a disabled person. Goods supplied in connection with (1) and (2) can be zero-rated.
3. The provision, installation and maintenance of equipment specially designed for domestic and personal use by a disabled person including hoists and stairlifts. Suppliers of such equipment will be aware of whether it can be zero-rated.

The following are examples of structural adaptations which can be carried out by housing authorities on their property. In addition improvement grants may be available for these adaptations.

General alterations. Extensions or alterations to provide bathroom, WC or bedroom with a level or suitably-ramped access.

Garaging and external facilities. Widening of garden paths, carport and/or undercover access to a dwelling if practical, remote control garage door opener to an existing garage which is used by a disabled driver.

Approaches to entrance doors. A fixed ramp in place of steps, modification of steps such as incorporating a half step or widening treads, handrails or balustrading to ramps or steps – both at an entrance or in other parts of a dwelling where necessary, doorcall and entryphone systems.

Doors and windows. Widening or re-hanging of doors to permit wheelchair manoeuvre, the installation of sliding or bi-fold doors in place of side hung doors, suitable ironmongery such as lever handles pull handles and rails to doors, kicking plates, protective edging to door frames, remote-control window openers, conversion of a window to a French window where there is no other wheelchair access to the garden, alterations to windows to give a satisfactory view for people in wheelchairs, larger windows for visually-impaired people.

Staircases and vertical circulation. Additional handrail to a staircase, a gate at the head or foot of the stairs, a stairlift, a vertical home lift or hoist.

Water services. Substitution of lever taps for screw-down taps, re-fixing taps at a convenient level, provision of remote-control valves for taps, provision of thermostatic control for showers, re-location of a control valve for the mains water supply.

Electrical and heating services. Re-fixing of socket outlets at a convenient level, the provision of additional socket outlets, rocker light switches, alarm call, a loud bell for people who are hard of hearing, re-location or prepayment meters, re-location of thermostat or heating controls, re-location of main switches for gas or electricity, central heating, or supplementary radiators to existing installations, fixed heating appliances either gas or electricity in place of an open fire or other solid fuel appliances, fluorescent lights in the kitchen, bathroom and working areas and visual door units for people who have impaired hearing, provision of a power supply for an electric hoist suspended from a ceiling track.

Provision of lifting equipment. Re-inforcement of ceilings for the provision of tracking for a personal hoist.

Acoustic installation. For example, in the instance when a family has an exceptionally noisy and disruptive child.

Entrance hall. Provision of a letter cage or delivery shelf, the re-location of a clothes hanging rail.

Kitchens. Alterations to provide fixed storage units, worktops and sink units at convenient levels, built-in cooker for use by a disabled person, provision of a waste-disposal unit to a sink.

Bathrooms and WCs. Shower unit in place of, or to supplement a bath, provision of a shower cubicle, provision of a suitable bath,

WC or washbasin, provision of a bidet or sluice sink, a fixed bath hoist, support rails to walls, raising of the WC fixture.

Storage. Storage provision for a wheelchair

PROCEDURE FOR CARRYING OUT ADAPTATIONS

Adaptations and the problems they are meant to overcome will differ from client to client, but the procedure for work is much the same in each instance.

1. Following a referral, the occupational therapist will carry out an initial interview and thorough assessment of the client. If it is felt that the physical environment inhibits a client's independence and alteration or adaptation to the home will help, the architect will need to be contacted, provided the client is in agreement.
2. A brief must be prepared for the architect by the therapist. This must include the following information:

   - Name, address, age of the client
   - Number living in the household, their ages and relationship with the client
   - Type of dwelling occupied and details of ownership
   - Problems experienced by the client, his physical limitations and likely prognosis
   - Equipment currently used to promote independence, including dimensions of walking equipment and wheelchair where necessary
   - Clear details of the problem experienced by the client

   It must be remembered that most architects are not fully aware of the handicapping effect of disability. Therefore the brief should be as clear as possible; nothing must be left to assumption or chance.
3. A further visit to the client's home together with the architect should be arranged so that the architect can assess the situation first hand, meet the client and his family and discuss proposals. The architect will also measure relevant areas within the home and carry out an inspection of the condition of the property, for example, the condition of a ceiling if an electric track hoist is to be fitted, or the suitability of a wall to bear weight if rails are to be fitted.

4. Following the visit, the architect will prepare a sketch plan which gives an overall picture of the scheme. This is passed to the occupational therapist for comment. Practice in this will make the therapist more conversant with reading drawings and using a scale rule to check dimensions. However, if there are any doubts or if the therapist does not understand particular aspects of the scheme, it is important that she discuss them with the architect before proceeding any further.

5. The client and his family should be visited again for further discussions, to make any necessary revisions to plans and to obtain their consent. Often the agreed scheme is the most economical one which can answer the client's needs. If the property is rented, the agreement of the landlord must also be obtained before taking the scheme any further.

6. Following an estimate of the cost, the EHO visits the client in order to discuss and determine the grant which is most applicable and to explain the procedure for application for the grant.

7. When the scheme has been agreed, a contract is drawn up. This gives details of the date the scheme is due to commence and the completion date. There are also clauses for non-completion dates with reference to compensation. If building regulation confirmation or planning permission is required, then the contract states who is responsible for obtaining these. Furthermore, it will confirm that the builder is sufficiently insured to cover any losses or damages incurred to persons or property during the course of the contract, how alterations to the contract will be agreed and a statement of the conditions under which the contract can be terminated either by the builder or the client. Reference is made to British Standards and codes of practice regarding the standards of workmanship and materials to be used.

8. Following this, the builder can start work. The architect is usually responsible for briefing the builder, but, in some instances this might be the responsibility of the therapist. Instructions must be clear and unambiguous. Measurements must be precise and correct in order to avoid unnecessary mistakes which can be costly and time consuming. Unless the client is controlling the contract, instructions can only be given to the builder by the architect or another named approved person. This point must be clearly explained to the client.

9. All work must be reviewed regularly by the therapist who must

Metrication

Although metrication was introduced into Great Britain some years ago, there is still some resistance to adopting the system fully.

The building industry only recognizes metres (m) and millimetres (mm); neither centimetres nor imperial measurements are acceptable. Occupational therapists therefore must understand the metric system to enable them to communicate with and understand builders, architects and other workers:

- On a plan, one metre is written as 1,000 mm
- One inch is equal to 25.4 mm, but for convenience this is usually reduced to 25 mm. Thus, 100 mm is equal to four inches, 300 mm is equal to one foot and one metre is equal to 39 inches
- A standard door width of two feet nine inches can be converted to 825 mm

A conversion table is helpful for quick reference:

Metric millimetres	Imperial feet and inches
25	1″
50	2″
75	3″
100	4″
150	6″
225	9″
300	1′0″
375	1′3″
450	1′6″
600	2′0″
750	2′6″
900	3′0″
1 200	4′0″
1 500	5′0″
1 800	6′0″
1 950	6′6″

With practice it becomes easier to understand the purpose of various types of architectural drawings. However it is important to be very clear about the function of the building to be constructed or adapted and to establish the needs of the people to be accommodated. Their functional requirements are paramount and must be borne in mind.

If there are points which are not clear or understood by the therapist, or if there are doubts about the effectiveness of the scheme, then it is vital that she seeks an explanation or further guidance from the architect.

Admitting ignorance is not an indication of stupidity. No architect will resent giving advice and information. It is the sign of a better professional to question whilst ideas are still on paper. Once construction has started changes will be expensive or impossible.

SOURCES OF INFORMATION (ADAPTATIONS)

If adaptations to property are to be undertaken by the social service department then the expertise of an architect will be available through the department. Some disabled people however may prefer to arrange adaptations to their property themselves. They may contact the occupational therapist for advice regarding details of organizations, architects or specialist bodies who might help. The organizations discussed below offer help to disabled individuals, groups or professional workers.

Access Committee for England

The aim of this committee is to achieve a more accessible environment for people with disabilities, either physical, sensory or mental. The Committee works towards the removal of physical and attitudinal barriers which prevent full participation in the life of society.

The major areas of work are firstly, legislation and practice. The committee advises government and other agencies on new legislation and its implementation. It also works in close association with professional institutions to further good practice in achieving accessible environments.

Furthermore, the committee provides support, information and advice to local access groups.

There are publications and a newsletter. In addition, seminars are organized regularly both at national and regional levels.

Centre on Environment for the Handicapped (CEH)

CEH provides an impartial architectural advisory service. There is a panel of architects who specialize in, or have experience of, designing for disabled people.

CEH can help enquirers by putting them in touch with local architects. A regional list of architects has been compiled. This includes brief notes on the type of work they have carried out.

Disabled people must contact the architect of their choice independently and discuss fees and contracts directly with them.

Other services offered by CEH include a register of recent buildings which make provision for handicapped people. The buildings included in the register are housing and group homes, sheltered housing, residential homes, hostels, day centres, schools, colleges, public buildings and places of recreation.

Another register is available which lists housing which offers care support for physically handicapped people.

CEH has a reference library and information service, regularly publishes material including a quarterly journal and runs a programme of seminars on selected topics concerned with the environment and handicapped people.

Disabled Living Foundation (DLF)

The DLF has a consultant architect who will give advice or comment on plans.

Royal Association for Disability and Rehabilitation (RADAR)

RADAR offers a service similar to the DLF.

Royal Institute of British Architects (RIBA)
Client's Advisory Service

RIBA has details of architects in particular geographical areas who have experience in designing and adapting buildings for disabled people. Information can be obtained either by writing or telephoning RIBA.

REFERENCES AND FURTHER READING

Armitage, J. (1983) *Barriers: A Survey of Housing, Physical Disability and the Role of Local Authorities*. Shelter.

Bristow, A.K. and Rutherford, A. (1980) *Islington: A Survey of Housing Designed for People who have a Physical Disability*. Department of the Environment.

British Standards Institute (1978) *Code of Practice for Design of Housing For the Convenience of Disabled People*. BS5619.

British Standards Institution (1979) *Code of Practice for Access for the Disabled to Buildings*. BS5810.

Centre on Environment for the Handicapped – design sheets. Centre on Environment for the Handicapped (1980).

Centre on Environment for the Handicapped (1981). *Housing Adaptations for Disabled People – Architectural Practicalities*. Report of a seminar, 26 February 1981.

Centre on Environment for the Handicapped (1982) *Housing Adaptations for Disabled People*. Report of a seminar, 14 October 1982.

Centre on Environment for the Handicapped (1982) *The Practicalities of House Adaptations for Disabled People*.

Cheshire County Council Department of Architecture (1980) *Made to Measure. Domestic Extensions and Adaptations for Physically Handicapped People*.

Department of the Environment (1978). Circular 59/78. *Adaptations of Housing for People who are Physically Handicapped*. HMSO

Department of the Environment. Circular 36/81. *Housing Acts 1974 and 1980: House Renovation Grants for the Disabled*.

Goldsmith, S. (1984) *Designing for the Disabled*, 4th Edn. Royal Institute of British Architects.

HMSO (1980) *Housing Act 1980*.

HMSO (1970) *Housing for Old People with Design Standards for the Disabled*.

Langton-Lockton, S. and Purcell, R. (1983) *Buying or Adapting a House or Flat: A Consumer Guide for Disabled People*. Centre of Environment for the Handicapped.

Lifchez, R. and Winslow, B. (1980) *Design for Independent Living: The Environment and Physically Disabled People*. Architectural Press.

Lockhart, T. (1981) *Housing Adaptations for Disabled People*. Disabled Living Foundation.

Thorpe, S. (1985) *Access for Disabled People. Design Guidance Notes for Developers*. Access Committee for England.

7

Alternative housing and living schemes

In some instances dwellings, because of their design, are unsuitable for adaptation. In other cases adaptations may be possible, but because of the amount of work required to render them suitable for disabled people, will be extremely costly and therefore impractical. If individual ability is not to be curtailed due to living in an inaccessible property, then alternative accommodation may need to be considered.

Sometimes people are reluctant to move house if this means they have to leave their immediate neighbourhood. This could be because there are close family ties, valuable friends and neighbours, a reliable GP or home help.

Children may not want to move school or a wage earner may have a job which prevents a move. Elderly people particularly may find moving house a traumatic experience if they have lived in their present property for many years. They will have memories, contacts and relationships which they might not want to leave behind in spite of the opportunity to move from poor housing to a modern, warm and convenient alternative.

Very careful thought and discussion therefore will need to take place before a decision is finally made to move house. An ill-considered decision may cause suffering. The therapist must discuss all options with the client and his family.

The variety of suitably-adapted properties will vary widely from area to area and it is important that the therapist is familiar with the range and categories available, not only in the immediate vicinity, but also nationally so that clients are given clear information.

Often waiting lists for purpose-built or suitably-adapted accommodation are lengthy. In some instances it may even be several years before a disabled person has a chance of obtaining such a property.

It is therefore important to consider the nature of the disability suffered by a client and the prognosis. The family of a handicapped child, for example, may be able to cope in standard property now, but in the future as the child grows and as his needs change they may require very different accommodation. It may be necessary to put names forward as early as possible for inclusion on waiting lists.

Local authorities, housing associations and voluntary organizations are concerned with the provision of special needs housing and residential accommodation for disabled people. Such housing is categorized under certain headings and the therapist will need to be aware of the features distinguishing each type of housing so that she is able to give accurate information to clients.

These include the following.

MOBILITY HOUSING

Mobility housing was introduced in a Department of the Environment (DOE) paper, in 1974. It is sometimes called 'general needs housing' and has not been designed specifically for disabled people. Certain features have been incorporated in the design to make it suitable for some ambulant disabled people or for wheelchair users who are able to stand to transfer from and to a wheelchair and to walk a few steps.

In addition mobility housing can be easily modified to suit particular disabilities without major structural adaptations.

The essential features which must be present in this type of housing are:

- The entrance must be level or have a ramp and the threshold must be flush. If a ramped approach is provided then there should be a level platform at the top which prevents a wheelchair user from rolling backwards when opening the door.
- The entrance and the entrances to principal rooms must have door sets of 900 mm, that is, the clear opening width must not be less than 775 mm. This makes them accessible for wheelchairs.
- The circulation space connecting the principal rooms must be 900 mm in width.
- The toilet must be on the same level as the entrance.
- If the house is a two-storey design then the staircase must have a straight flight and there must be a circulation space of at least 900 × 900 mm at the top and bottom of the stairs. This allows

for a stair lift to be installed, so that a disabled person can reach the upper rooms of the house if they are unable to climb the stairs.

- A lift must be available to provide access to flats above ground floor level. the minimal internal measurements of the lift car must be 1400 mm in depth and 1100 mm wide.

Other features which may be incorporated into the design of wheelchair housing include:

- The convenient location and design of light switches, socket outlets and heating facilities.
- There should be careful specification of window and door furniture. For example, door handles should be easy to grip and involve minimal finger movement.
- Walls should be suitable for load-bearing grab rails.
- Kitchen and bathroom fitments should be planned to take into account the needs of people with disabilities.
- Floor coverings should be non-slip; pile of carpets should not be so deep as to impede wheelchair manoeuvring.

Examples of wheelchair housing are bungalows, ground-floor flats in low-rise blocks of flats, two-storey houses with the bedroom and bathroom at ground-floor level, flats with lifts to the upper levels, and two-storey houses with straight flights of stairs.

WHEELCHAIR HOUSING

Wheelchair housing has been designed for wheelchair users who are unable to walk or to stand in order to transfer from or into the wheelchair.

Overall, wheelchair housing is more spacious than mobility housing. For example, a two-bedroomed flat, normally allocated to three people, may be allocated to two people if one uses a wheelchair.

The Department of the Environment introduced this type of housing in a paper, (2/75) in 1975, and specified the following features:

- Entrances should be either level or have a slightly ramped approach. There should be no threshold obstruction.
- Internally there should be space to allow wheelchairs to be manoeuvred easily. Thus, passageways should be 1200 mm wide

and there should be door sets of 900 mm with a clear opening width of 775 m.

- Kitchens should be planned to allow wheelchair manoeuvre. Equipment and storage should be accessible. Work surfaces should be low with knee space underneath. Sinks should be shallow and wall cupboards low.
- Showers and baths should be planned for wheelchair use. Shower areas should be without steps, and baths should have a transfer platform at the head.
- There should be sufficient space within the toilet area to allow transfer from a wheelchair.
- Fittings including window controls, door furniture, electrical sockets and switches should be placed so that they can be reached from a wheelchair. They should be easy to grasp with minimal finger movements.
- Window heights should be such that views are not restricted from a wheelchair.
- Ceilings need to be sufficiently strong to take the weight of a ceiling track electric hoist if necessary.
- If a carport is provided then access between it and the dwelling needs to be covered and level.

Consideration needs to be given to accessibility to local community facilities such as shops, libraries, the post office, and so on.

SHELTERED HOUSING

The concept of sheltered housing varies widely, but usually it is a term used to refer to a group of purpose-built or converted dwellings fitted with an alarm call system and served by a resident warden. Sheltered housing schemes are available for people of varying ages. Provision for such housing is usually made by local authorities and housing associations. Some private schemes however are now available.

Generally speaking, sheltered housing is intended for people who, with practical help from domiciliary services such as community nursing, home help, meals on wheels and so on, are able to live in the community rather than in residential care.

Although a warden is available, her role is to provide background support rather than daily physical help. Residents live in their own self-contained units, but a communal room is usually available for use also.

PART III ACCOMMODATION

Part III accommodation is provided by local authorities for people in need of care and attention because of age and infirmity. The National Assistance Act of 1948, Part III, Section 21 (as amended by Section 195 and Schedule 23 of the Local Government Act 1972, and Section IV of Social Work Scotland Act 1968 for Scotland) made it a duty of local authorities to provide such accommodation. Some homes however are provided by voluntary and private organizations. The DSS guideline for residential home places is 25 places per 1000 population aged 65 years and over. Admission criteria is that residents should be mobile, continent and able to dress and feed themselves. However, elderly people in residential homes are often more dependent and infirm than many of the homes were originally designed or staffed for. Some homes have been set up to help mentally infirm elderly people. In other homes, a percentage of residents suffer from some degree of mental confusion.

The number of single and shared rooms in Part III homes varies although couples are usually given a room of their own. Sometimes people are able to bring along selected items of furniture with them from their own homes. Dining rooms, sitting rooms, bathrooms and WCs are communal. Facilities and privacy varies between homes as does level of staffing and the amount of activity within the home.

Great care should be taken when selecting Part III accommodation and it should be regarded potentially as a home for a person for the rest of his life. Unfortunately, in all too many instances, demand for places far outweighs the number of places available. It is often a case of taking what is available rather than being able to select carefully a home which is suited to the needs of the individual.

REMAINING AT HOME

A number of schemes are available which provide help to people living in their own homes to enable them to continue to do so. Such schemes usually employ non-professional carers who offer a more flexible form of support than the statutory services are able to provide. Two examples of such schemes are the Crossroad Care Attendant Scheme and the Independent Living Scheme operated by Community Service Volunteers.

Crossroad Care Attendant Scheme

Crossroads is a registered charity which provides help to people caring for a physically or mentally handicapped person at any age living at home.

Help takes the form of care attendants who will visit families with a disabled member on a regular daily or weekly basis. Hours are flexible and an individual package of care can be offered. Such help can relieve stress in families or persons responsible for the care of disabled people, and in some instances, the scheme can help disabled people who live alone.

Care attendants work closely with statutory and voluntary organizations so that families receive carefully co-ordinated care. The aim of the scheme is to supplement and complement existing services, not to replace them.

Care attendants come from a variety of backgrounds; some have basic nursing experience, but all are mature and caring people.

Each Crossroads Scheme is autonomous, but is linked to the national association. A new scheme will only be formed if realistic funding is obtained from statutory sources for a minimum period of two years. This allows time for the scheme to become known and established in the area, and for its service to be evaluated for future funding. The association, through its development officers, will work closely with an area which is seeking to set up a Crossroads Scheme and offer guidance and help at all stages.

A part-time co-ordinator is responsible for the day-to-day running of the scheme, the supervision of care attendants, assessment of family needs and for supplying help at the times required by the family.

A management committee made up of representatives of health, social services, voluntary organizations, family practitioner and a carer or disabled person, is responsible for the policy making, finance and staffing of the scheme.

Referrals to the Crossroad Care Attendant Scheme can be made from any source.

Independent Living Scheme, Community Service Volunteers (CSV)

The CSV's Independent Living Scheme matches full-time volunteers with individuals and families who need a high and concentrated level of support to enable them to live in the community and to lead as independent a life as possible.

Some projects work on a contractural basis, running for a specific period of time. Others are longer term so that as one volunteer completes her period of service, arrangements are made for another to take her place.

The volunteers are usually aged between 16 and 35 years, from a variety of backgrounds though they are usually untrained. They can undertake physical care and other practical help in all aspects of daily life. On average, volunteers work for 40 hours per week, but where necessary the scheme can provide 24-hour care.

Projects are organized through and supported by local social service departments, health authorities or other statutory or voluntary agencies.

Volunteers must receive regular support from an external project supervisor. This is usually a social worker or other professional worker from the sponsoring agency.

A development fee is charged to the sponsoring agency when a new project is set up. A monthly placement fee is then charged for each volunteer. In addition, volunteers must be provided with pocket money, meals, accommodation, out of pocket expenses, suitable work/protective clothing and one week's paid holiday for every four months of service.

Independent Living Fund

This is a special fund for severely disabled people who can live at home if they have a great deal of paid help. Details and application forms from Independent Living Fund, Room 520, New Court, Carey Street, London WC2A 2L5.

REFERENCES AND FURTHER READING

Bennian, C. (1988) *A Study of People with Disabilities Living in Residential Accommodation to Independent Living.* Spastics Society, London.

Cantle, E.F. and Sharp, N.A. (1977) *Mobility Housing: More Flexibility in Housing for the Disabled.* Centre on Environment for the Handicapped.

Centre on Environment for the Handicapped (1979) *Mobility and Wheelchair Housing.* A report of a seminar held at the King's Fund Centre, 10 September 1979.

Community Service Volunteers (1988) *Independent Living in the 1990's: The*

Consumer's View. A submission from voluntary agencies to Sir Roy Griffiths review of community care. Community Service Volunteers, London.

Department of the Environment (1975) Housing Development Directorate
Occasional Paper 2/75 *Wheelchair Housing.* HMSO, London.

Department of the Environment (1977) *Wheelchair Housing: A survey of
Purpose-designed Dwellings for Disabled People.*

Department of the Environment (1984) Housing Development Directorate
Occasional Paper 2/74 *Mobility Housing.* HMSO, London.

Seed, P. and Montgomery, B. (1989) *Towards Independent Living: Issues
for Different Client Groups.* Jessica Kingsley, London.

Shearer, A. (1982) *Living Independently.* Centre on Environment and King's
Fund.

8

Access and circulation in the home

Most people live in a house which has not been designed to accommodate someone with a disability. Access and circulation in the home can therefore be severely restricted if a person has limited or no mobility and needs to use walking equipment or a wheelchair to get around.

It has already been stated that the problems experienced by every disabled person are particular to him and the environment in which he lives. Thus it is not possible to impose the same solution on each person. Whilst this is true, there are a number of points which need to be carefully considered if a home is to be adapted to allow easier access and circulation. Recommended dimensions are given below. These may be more helpful in public buildings which cater for the needs of a wide range of people. Adaptations in domestic dwellings should be installed to suit individual needs.

RAMPS

Steps at the entrance to a house may prevent the occupant from entering or leaving if he has mobility problems or uses a wheelchair. A ramped entrance will permit access, but ramps cannot be constructed in all instances. Essential dimensions to consider are as follows:

Gradient. The preferred gradient of the ramp is 1:20, no greater than 1:12. Some wheelchair users with particularly strong upper limbs may be able to negotiate steeper gradients independently, but these are hazardous particularly to ambulant disabled people, and should be avoided.

Width. The preferred width is 1200 mm although 900 mm is sometimes accepted. A width of 1800 mm allows wheelchairs to pass each other on the ramp.

Safety edges. These are required on each side of the ramp, a minimum of 40 mm high to prevent the wheelchair from slipping over the sides.

Length. Long, continuous ramps should be avoided, but where there is a high rise, level platforms with a minimum length of 1200 mm are required at every 4500 mm intervals, to allow the wheelchair user time to rest.

Rails. Hand rails are required on both sides of the ramp. They should be easy to grasp, 45–50 mm diameter. Nylon coated or hard wood rails are more comfortable than metal.

Surface. Ramp surfaces should be non-slip and fireproof. Untreated timber ramps should not be left out of doors as they can become slippery when wet. Portable ramps should be stored in a dry place when not in use.

Siting. Avoid bridging the damp-proof course – the architect or builder will advise on this. The ramp should be placed so that it does not obstruct a public right of way. The ramp should not be sited close to rough-surfaced walls in order to prevent people from hurting themselves or harming their wheelchair if they brush against it. Where the gradient would be too steep, a short-rise powered lifting platform might be considered as an option.

DOORS

1. There should be a minimum clear opening width of 750–800 mm. However, if a wheelchair is used it's overall dimensions will need to be checked to ensure that it can pass through the doorway with ease. Sometimes rehanging the door so that it opens in the opposite direction allows easier access.
2. Projecting thresholds should be avoided if possible, as they act as an obstruction. Some wheelchair users might be able to negotiate a low threshold (20 mm) if the edges are chamfered. A range of flexible thresholds fixed to the floor and with a

retracting cushion are available for interior and outdoor use.

3. A kicking plate with a minimum width of 400 mm will help in preventing the lower part of the door from being damaged by a wheelchair or walking equipment. These plates are usually made from plastic or aluminium.

4. A sliding door might be considered if space is limited or if a hinged door will impede access or wheelchair circulation, but the door width must be adequate to allow the user through with walking equipment or a wheelchair. A sliding door must be easy to operate and not stick or slide off its track.

5. If grip is poor then a lever handle might be most suitable. It should have a minimum diameter of 20mm and a length of 250 mm. It should be fixed at a height of approximately 1040 mm above the base of the door. Moulded lever handles which fit the hand comfortably are also helpful. Round handles offer an inadequate grip for most people. If the client uses a wheelchair then an additional pull handle will assist in closing the door. This should have a maximum diameter of 35 mm and be of a length of 300 mm. Like the standard door handle it should be fixed 1000 mm from the base of the door. There should be a gap of 45 mm between the handle and the door to ensure that the user's hand can grasp it comfortably.

CIRCULATION SPACE

Circulation space for wheelchair users should be unobstructed. Appliances and fittings such as radiators should be recessed if space is limited to prevent destruction. Corridors and passages should have a minimum width of 1200 mm to allow wheelchair manoeuvre. Problems of manoeuvre might arise if several doors open off the same corridor. Dimensions will need to be carefully checked to ensure that the wheelchair user can move easily from one room to another (see Tables 8.1 and 8.2).

STAIRS

If the person is mobile, but has some difficulty in mounting and descending stairs an extra rail may be required. The rail should have a diameter of between 45 and 50 mm. It should be fixed at a height of 850 mm above the nosing line of the stair. Stair rails should be

Table 8.1 Wheelchairs – seat widths and overall widths. A quick guide to measurements (given in inches and centimetres)

Pushchairs

	9LJ	9L	10	12 Avon-de-luxe	Light-weight (Newton)	13C	13J	Andrews Maclaren Buggy Major	Carters Hemi-plegic Chair	Everest & Jennings transit Chairs	Meyra Rehab transit Chairs	Ortho-kinetics Alvema	Vessa Variant Transit
Seat width (minimum)	13 (33)	17 (43)	15 (38)	12 (30)	13¾ (35)	12 (30.5)	15 (38)	15½ (39)	16 (41)	16 (41)	15 (38)	17 (43)	14 (36)
Seat width (maximum)	16 (40.6)	19 (48)	17 (43)	16 (41)	16¾ (42.5)	12 (30.5)	20 (51)	15½ (39)	18 (46)	18 (46)	18¾ (48)	17 (43)	19 (48)
Overall width	24 (61)	26 (66)	24 (61)	22-23 (56-58)	23-25 (59-64)	22 (56)	22-27 (56-59)	21 (54)	24-26 (60-65)	21-26 (53-65)	25 (63)		23-28 (58-70)

Self-propelled chairs

	1J	1	3J	3	7	8LJ	8BL	8L	Alton	Ashington	Corby	Rossi Sprint	Hemi-plegic Jennings Universal	Everest & Newton Light-weight
Seat width (minimum)	15 (38)	18 (46)	15 (38)	18 (46)	13 (33)	16 (41)	17 (43)	16 (41)	16 (41)	14 (35.5)	16 (41)	16 (41)	16 (41)	13¾ (35)
Seat width (maximum)	15 (38)	18 (46)	15 (38)	18 (46)	15 (38)	16 (41)	18 (46)	18 (46)	16 (41)	14 (35.5)	16 (41)	18 (46)	17 (47)	16¾ (42.5)
Overall width	22 (56)	25 (64)	23½ (60)	26½ (67)	24 (61)	23 (58)	23 (58)	25 (64)	23 (58)	24 (61)	21 (53)	23 (58)	24-26 (60-65)	24-26 (60-65)

Table 8.2 Indoor power chairs. Dimensions in inches and centimetres

Width	BEC 3	BEC 8	BEC 14	BEC 16	BEC 17	BEC 20	BEC 24
Seat width (minimum)	14 (36)	14 (36)	14 (36)	14 (36)	14 (36)	14 (36)	14 (36)
Seat width (maximum)	17 (43)	17 (43)	17 (43)	17 (43)	17 (43)	17 (43)	17 (43)
Overall width	25 (64)	25 (64)	25 (64)	25 (64)	22 (56)	25 (64)	25 (64)

smooth and continuous and should continue for a further 300 mm (450 mm preferably) at the top and bottom of the stairs to indicate that there has been a change of level. Here, the rail should be 1000 mm above floor level. The position of the rail needs to be clearly marked on the wall so that whoever is to secure it knows exactly where it needs to be fixed. Before deciding on a rail however, it must be established that the load bearing wall is sufficiently strong to take it. A batten or cleat may be necessary to reinforce the wall. The builder will advise on this.

If there is still inability to climb and descend stairs, yet access is required to rooms above ground-floor level possibly because a ground floor extension may not be feasible, or alternative housing is unacceptable or unavailable, then the provision of a stair climber or home lift may be an alternative and these are described below.

Stair climbers

The British Standard Document, *Powered Stair Lifts* (BS5776: 1979) gives consideration to the design of stair climbers, building requirements, technical specifications, the testing, inspection and servicing of the stair climber and guidance to purchasers. Even if clients propose to buy and install the equipment themselves, they should be guided in their selection by the therapist who can point out the requirements of the BSI.

Consideration of the following points may be helpful before installing a stair climber.

1. *Models available*. Although design varies, there are basically

three types of stair climber:

- for standing passengers
- for seated passengers
- for wheelchair passengers

Some models will only climb a straight flight of stairs including a landing. Others can negotiate 50° or 180° turnings. Usually a track is fixed to the side of the stairs and this carries the seat or platform up and down the length of the stairs. Different controls are available: push-button, constant pressure or remote control and the choice will depend very much on the ability of the user.

Building regulation approval is not necessary for the installation of a stair climber unless it is being fitted in a house under construction.

2. *Prognosis of the condition suffered.* Will the model to be installed be of use in the future? For example, if someone is suffering from a condition which is likely to deteriorate to the extent that they will require a wheelchair for mobility in the future, it may be wiser to consider the installation of a lift with a wheelchair platform rather than a standing platform.

3. *Type of staircase.* Is it wide enough to accommodate a stair climber? Does the width of the stairway leave sufficient space for safe use by others in the family after the tracking has been installed? The effective width of the staircase may be reduced by up to one-third, although it is normally possible to fold seats and platforms in order to free the stairs for conventional use. The track should not prevent the opening of doors and access to cupboards and windows. Whether the stairs are straight or curved and if there is a quarter landing must be noted as this will determine the type of equipment to be purchased.

4. *Landing.* Is there sufficient space at the top and bottom of the stairs to allow transfer on and off the stair climber? If a wheelchair platform carriage is used, the dimensions need to be checked to ensure there is sufficient space. The landing should be free from projections, holes and indeed anything which is likely to cause injury.

5. *Trappings.* Trappings such as low ceilings giving insufficient headroom, or windows along the staircase which might be hazardous, should be considered.

6. *Ability of the user*. Can the stair climber be used from a standing or seated position or will a wheelchair platform be required? Consider the ability to transfer from a wheelchair to a seat if a stair climber with a seat is to be installed. Check that the seat height is suitable. A seat belt or harness may be required. Duplicate walking equipment or a wheelchair may be required for use upstairs. The direction of travel should be considered. If the users knees are fixed in extension, for example, then sideways travel may be impossible. A grab rail may be required at the top of the stairs to help with transferring, to and from the stair climber.

7. *Controls*. Can these be operated by both right and left hand? Will there be a problem in operating a constant pressure switch? If so, some manufacturers are able to supply an alternative. If the controls cannot be operated by the user then an attendant will be required. If that is the case it will need to be decided where the controls will be placed; the top and bottom of the stairs, or hand-held. A lockable on/off switch may be required to restrict the use of the stair climber, thereby preventing possible accidents, especially if there are young children in the house.

8. *Lighting*. Is this adequate and are there switches at the top and bottom of the stairs?

9. *Noise*. This may be disturbing to neighbours if the house is in a terrace or is semi-detached. Sound insulation may need to be considered.

10. *Electricity supply*. Pre-payment meters should be avoided so that electricity does not cut out mid-journey.

11. *Alarm systems*. These should be considered for those living alone in case of stair-climber breakdown.

12. *Breakdown/maintenance servicing facilities*. The responsibility for maintenance needs to be clarified. Maintenance must be carried out regularly by a qualified engineer. A record of maintenance should be kept by the user with a name and contact number in case of emergency. It may be helpful to tape this to the wall beside the staircase for ease of access. Some authorities require that an indemnity form is signed by the user and therapist confirming that verbal and written instructions have been given regarding the safe use of a

particular stair climber. If authorities have contributed towards the cost of the stair climber then an agreement may have to be signed by the client stating that, if and when it is no longer required, then it should be made available for re-siting by the authority.

Usually stair climbers can be removed with a minimum of disruption.

Home lifts

Home lifts should comply to the British Standard Powered Homelifts (BS5900: 1980). Several firms manufacture a range of home lifts with a variety of features, but basically they are of two types:

- manually operated lifts
- electrically-operated lifts

The former, although less expensive, require much more effort to operate as there is a winch to activate the platform. It must be decided whether the user has the ability to carry out this activity or if there will be an attendant. Most home lifts do not need a shaft and can be fitted into a stairwell or inside room with a hole cut through the ceiling. If a complete shaft is to be constructed outside of the property then planning permission will be required.

Manufacturers can give guidance regarding this and will also give advice about the positioning of the lift inside a dwelling. A fire officer may need to be contacted if the lift makes any changes in the fire resistance of the upper floor.

If a home lift is to be installed then consideration should be given to the following:

Size of lift car: Is it solely for the user or will an attendant be required to travel also? Does the lift car allow for standing passengers, is there a seat or is there sufficient space to carry the user's wheelchair? Check the overall length of the wheelchair against the measurement of the inside of the lift car.

Access to lift car: Lifts are space consuming, thus the space available in the rooms served by the lift car must be considered as does the position of the car floor to the landing floor. It may be necessary to provide a ramped access.

Type of lift car: Some installations offer an exposed seat, others are boxed. It needs to be established whether the user can tolerate being confined within a totally enclosed car or if vision panels are needed. A harness or seat belt may be required for safety and security. If the lift car is of an open type, check that there are no projections which could strike the body in transit. Types of controls vary and the ability of the user must be borne in mind.

Alarm system: These are recommended for someone living alone or spending a good deal of time alone should an emergency or break-down occur. In case of breakdown the lift should be fitted with a failsafe brake system and a means of returning the lift car to the ground.

Electricity: Pre-payment electricity meters should be avoided.

Maintenance and breakdown facilities: The responsibility of maintenance needs to be clarified and regular maintenance needs to be carried out. A 24-hour number to contact in case of emergency should be readily accessible to the user. It is essential to give clear verbal and written instructions on the safe use of the lift. Authorities may request that an indemnity form be signed and which confirms this. It may also be necessary to sign a document agreeing to the re-siting of the lift when and if it is no longer required by the client. This will apply only if the item has been paid for by the authority.

ACCESS IN THE KITCHEN

Many people have an image of their ideal kitchen. It is one of the rooms in a home which offers enormous scope for detailed design. In many instances however, therapists are unlikely to be involved in a total overhaul of their clients' kitchens. They may have to re-arrange what is already there, owing to restrictions in space and funds. There are several points to consider when assessing the suitability of a kitchen for individual clients.

1. Use of the kitchen

It must be established if the kitchen is to be used by other people as well as the client. A compromise in design and layout may be necessary to accommodate the needs of several people. The function of the kitchen also needs to be determined. For example, is it to be used only for food preparation, will it be a dining kitchen or will it be used for several functions? The link between the kitchen and the rest of the house including the outside will need to be considered.

2. Access and circulation space

A larger floor space will be required for a wheelchair user. A minimum circulation space of 1200 mm will be required.

3. Layout

For ease of work and to minimize difficulties in balancing, carrying, moving and lifting items, work surfaces should ideally be continuous and, if possible, compact. Ideally, the sink and cooker should be close together with work surfaces on either side. The depth and height of work surfaces will need to be considered in relation to the person's ability to reach up, across and down. A wheelchair user will require space underneath work surfaces to allow close access to the surface. The model of wheelchair used will have a bearing on accessibility to work tops. For example, a wheelchair with desk arms or removable arms might make reaching easier than one with fixed full length arms.

4. Storage space

In order to minimize unnecessary moving around and consequent fatigue, items should be stored close to where they are required. High or deep shelves should be avoided as they are difficult for most people to reach. Extra fittings such as shelves on the back of cupboard doors or rotating shelves might help to overcome the problem of reaching into difficult places. Ease of operating doors, cupboards and drawers also needs to be considered.

5. Sink

Access to the sink and taps needs to be checked. Standard taps may need to be replaced with lever taps if hand function is limited. A single-lever mixer tap which has a swivel arm might enable a person to fill kettles and saucepans on a work top rather than lift them out of a sink. The tap will need to be carefully positioned at the rear or side of the bowl to allow this.

6. Sockets and switches

Careful siting of these is important so that they are accessible.

7. Cookers

Numerous models are available and very careful consideration must be given so that the model selected can be used fully and effectively. If there is sufficient space and funds, a separate hob and oven can be installed at the most effective height for the user. The positioning of controls, their grip, the height of the grill, access to the oven, ease of cleaning and the height of the cooker in relation to work surfaces are some of the points to consider when selecting a cooker. If grip is poor and controls are difficult to operate, alternative controls are available. Both the gas and electricity companies employ home economists who will advise. Alternatives to standard cookers might be worth considering such as microwave ovens, slow cookers and electric frying pans. These are often a less expensive way of solving a problem rather than buying a new cooker.

8. Fridges and fridge/freezers

Similar considerations need to be made when selecting a fridge or freezer. Ease of defrosting is important.

9. Washing machines and dryers

Automatic washing machines reduce handling of heavy wet washing. The person's ability to stand or stoop will affect the choice of a top loading or front loading machine. Some automatic washing machines may have an integral tumble drying facility. Controls should be accessible and easily managed.

REFERENCES AND FURTHER READING

British Standards Institution (1979). *Specification for Powered Stair Lifts*. BS5776.

British Standards Institution (1980) *Specification for Powered Homelifts* BS5900.

Centre on Environment for the Handicapped (1984) *Adapting Kitchens for Disabled People*.

Centre on Environment for the Handicapped (1984) *Stairlifts and Home Lifts for Disabled People*.

Rennie, A. and Galer, M. (eds) (1981) *Ergonomics of Cooker Design*. Institute for Consumer Ergonomics.

Washing machines (including suitability for use by people with various disabilities), *Which?* (January, 1989), 446–1170.

9

Leisure

Assessment of a disabled person's ability to carry out leisure activities can be overlooked by the occupational therapist when trying to assist people to cope with vital daily living skills such as toiletting, bathing and eating. However, the occupational therapist is often the best person to initiate or guide people towards appropriate leisure or social outlets. These activities have an important place in every one's life and perhaps more so nowadays when so many people, disabled and non disabled, have difficulty in finding gainful employment.

It is important to establish the client's interests. He may have been actively involved in a particular sport, hobby or pastime prior to the onset of his disability or illness, but he may feel that his present physical limitations prevent him from continued involvement. Lack of confidence becomes a major stumbling block. There are numerous clubs and organizations covering every aspect of leisure, sports, physical recreation, hobbies, pastimes, the arts and specific disability action groups (eg. stroke clubs) both on a national and local basis. Most welcome beginners as well as more advanced participants. Not all organizations have been set up specifically for disabled people and not all disabled people will choose to mix solely with people suffering from conditions similar to their own.

Local adult education programmes may be offered on a whole range of subjects, not only leisure and social pursuits. They may also offer a chance to improve education or to learn a particular skill. Many people will benefit from the opportunity to move outside their usual environment though others will prefer to carry out leisure activities at home. So much depends on individual preference and ability.

Many organizations provide details of accessible facilities and these must be considered if mobility is limited. Internal access, showers, changing rooms, toilets, fire escapes, lifts, internal circulation, acoustics, communication including sign posting, hazards and obstacles, should be considered.

The client may wish to join or form a local disability action group. The function of these groups varies, some having a highly political profile reflecting local need. Others may organize social events and Dial-a-Ride schemes.

TRANSPORTATION

Independent travel outside the home will prove difficult or even impossible for some people. However, some means of getting about must be sought if a person wishes to take part in activities outside the home. Many areas now operate a dial-a-ride scheme or similar service. Details of availability and cost are normally available through social service departments. Other people may wish to travel independently and drive their own vehicle. Driving instruction can be arranged for people with disabilities. There are several centres which have facilities for assessing a person's ability to drive and of the range of controls and equipment needed to help overcome any physical limitations. In addition, some driving schools offer disabled people lessons in adapted cars. The Disabled Drivers' Association has area representatives who will introduce potential drivers to someone in their locality who has a similar disability. Hand controls can be fitted to most types of automatic and manual cars to suit individual requirements. Some are in kit form and these have the advantage that they can be removed if the car is to be exchanged or sold. Power-assisted steering conversions and joystick steering are also available as are hand brake conversions.

Driving licences

The minimum age for driving a car is 17 years. However, people in receipt of the mobility allowance may start driving at the age of 16. The 1972 Road Traffic Act refers to certain disabilities, whose sufferers may have their licence refused, revoked or limited. These are: epilepsy, severe subnormality or mental deficiency, liability to sudden attacks of disabling giddiness or fainting resulting from any disorder or defect of the heart or any other cause, and inability to read the number plate of a vehicle at a specified distance. If a handicapped person wishes to apply for a licence, a medical examination is required by the Driver and Vehicle Licensing Centre.

Orange Badge Scheme

Car parking close to a chosen destination can sometimes be difficult. The provision of an orange badge may help. An applicant must be disabled, but can either be the driver or a passenger, including a child over two years of age. People eligible to apply include: visually handicapped people; a person suffering from a permanent disability which causes considerable difficulty in walking; a person in receipt of the mobility allowance. Applications for the badge are made through social service departments.

HOLIDAYS AND OUTINGS

Many social service departments and voluntary organizations arrange holidays and outings for groups of disabled people of all ages and suffering from various disabilities. They are rarely provided without charge, but may be subsidized, the amount depending on personal income. Such holidays have the advantage that escorts are provided and suitable transport is arranged, sometimes from door to door. Accommodation is usually accessible and often equipment such as hoists, stairlifts, adapted toilets and showers are available. In some instances, special diets may be catered for. Applications are made through local social service departments.

Not all disabled people, however, wish to travel in a group with other disabled people. It is possible to arrange individual holidays, but some forward planning is advisable.

The following information may be helpful:

1. Royal Association for Disability and Rehabilitation (RADAR), the RAC and the AA publish annual handbooks giving details of suitable holiday accommodation including details of self-catering and special interest holidays in the United Kingdom, Eire and overseas countries. The AA guide covers facilities in motorway service areas, accessible public toilets and places to visit.

2. Access guides to many towns are available including some

overseas. These are available from the RADAR Holidays Officer. Some tourist boards produce their own access guides.

3. A comprehensive access guide to toilets in England and Wales is available from RADAR. The organization also operates a National Key Scheme (NKS) for toilets for disabled people. In order to counter vandalism in public toilets, many authorities and some organizations in the UK have fitted standard locks to toilets designated for disabled users. On payment of a small fee to RADAR, a key is issued which fits the locks. RADAR issues and regularly updates a list of toilets covered by the NKS.

4. If journeys using public transport are to be made, it is advisable to forewarn the appropriate authorities in advance so that arrangements can be made regarding access, seating and so on. Guides to railways and airports are available.

General points

If therapists are involved in planning or giving advice to clients regarding holidays, consideration must be given to transporting any equipment which is normally required for day-to-day independence. Portable, folding or lightweight models of some items are available, such as commodes, toilet seats and wheelchairs. A department may find it worthwhile to keep a small stock of such equipment which can be loaned out to clients for the duration of their holiday. If the traveller has problems of continence, protective equipment including a mattress cover if necessary, should be included with holiday luggage.

REFERENCES AND FURTHER READING

Education/Employment

Bookis, J., in conjunction with RADAR (1984)
Beyond the School Gate. A Study of Disabled Young People Aged 13–19. RADAR.
Heginbotham, C. (1984) *Webbs and Mazes. Approaches to Care in the Community.* Centre on Environment for the Handicapped.
Paediatric Research Unit (1985) Royal Devon and Exeter Hospitals. *The Needs of Handicapped Young Adults.* First Report.

Library Services Trust (1988) *Can't See to Read? Resources for Visually Handicapped People.* 5th ed. Library Association, London.

Leisure, recreational pursuits and holidays

Attenborough Report (1985). *Arts and Disabled People.* Bedford Square Press.

Centre of Environment for the Handicapped (1981). *Gardens and Grounds for Disabled and Elderly People.*

Leisure Information Service List 6, Disabled Living Foundation.

National Gardens Scheme (published annually). *Gardens of England and Wales Open to the Public.* National Gardens Scheme, London.

Pearson, A. (1985) *Arts for Everyone: Guidance on Provision for Disabled People.* Centre on Environment for the Handicapped.

Royal Association for Disability and Rehabilitation (RADAR) (1984) *Access to Public Conveniences: A Comprehensive Guide for England and Wales.*

Royal Association for Disability and Rehabilitation. *Holidays for Disabled People.* Annually.

Royal Association for Disability and Rehabilitation. *Holidays and Travel Abroad.* Annually.

Sutherland, A. and Soames, P. (1984) *Adventure Play with Handicapped Children.* Souvenir Press.

Thomas, N. (1984) *Sports and Recreation Provision for Disabled People.* Disabled Living Foundation.

Thomson, N. (1984) Dendy, E. and de Deney, D. (eds) *Sports and Recreation Provision for Disabled People.* Disabled Living Foundation.

Toilet equipment

Page, M., Cooper, S. and Feeney, R. (1981) *The Selection of Toilet Aids for Disabled Persons. Results of an Evaluation Study and Guidelines for the Section of Toilet Aids for Adult Disabled People.* Institute for Consumer Ergonomics.

Transport

Buchanan, J.M. (1982) *The Mobility of Disabled People in a Rural Environment.* RADAR.

Buchanan, J. and Chamberlain, A. (1978) *The Mobility of Disabled People in an Urban Environment.* RADAR.

Darbrough, A. and Kinrade, D. (1985) *Motoring and Mobility for Disabled People.* RADAR.

Wheelchairs

British Red Cross Society (1983) *People in Wheelchairs – Hints for Helpers*.
Disabled Living Foundation. *Method of Loading a Wheelchair into a 2-Door Car*.

10

Record keeping and reporting

Pressure of work and the demands placed on a therapist to provide a service to handicapped people may cause her to neglect routine record keeping and report and letter writing.

Few people have complete recall. Unless notes are written up as soon as possible after contact, important facts will be forgotten, as will tasks which the therapist had agreed to undertake. Not only will individual credibility be lost, but poor record keeping reflects badly on a whole department.

If they are handwritten, notes must be legible. Each entry must be dated and signed and additional sheets should have the client's name and case number clearly printed on them in case they become detached. It is helpful to keep individual sets of notes in plastic or card folders or polythene bags. This system keeps an individual's notes together, apart from other peoples' and avoids loss. There are various ways of recording information and departments differ in the method they adopt. Whatever method is used, however, it should be systematic, allowing other colleagues to retrieve the following information about clients.

1. Demographic data: name, address, telephone number so that the client can be clearly identified.
2. Name of the therapist responsible for the client.
3. Dates of all the visits.
4. Details of the visits; standard assessment forms are useful for a quick appraisal of a person's ability. A summary of the situation, a list of problems experienced by the client, the action required to solve the problem, and the date action was taken should all be included.
5. Details and dates of any telephone calls made or received directly

or in connection with the client.

6. Copies of reports, letters or any other documentation relevant to the client. A colour-coding system may be used for easy identification of paperwork between specific departments.

If notes are removed from the filing system a tracer card should be left in their place so that they can be traced should an enquiry arise.

It should be possible, using the information recorded, to evaluate the service given, particularly the time taken to deliver the service. Such information is important. It accounts for use of the therapist's time, and may be used as a lever to attempt to improve the service.

Separate brief notes of equipment issued and adaptations carried out, cross-referenced with the main case notes, are helpful for quick reference. This may be necessary should a hazard notice be issued about a certain piece of equipment which then must be recalled for repair or re-issue. This system is also a useful means of recording the amount of equipment issued or adaptations carried out to date.

Accurate records are essential evidence for the therapist or the employing authority, should a client bring an action for damages.

Some therapists find dictating machines a useful means of recording details of the visit immediately after it has taken place. Tape recording can be used in two ways:

1. The salient points of the assessment can be recorded and then used later as a prompt when the therapist writes the case notes in full.
2. If the therapist has good secretarial support with audio typing, case notes can be typed up directly from the tape. For this to succeed, facts must be dictated fully and systematically if they are to make sense on paper.

Dictating is a skill worth acquiring. When mastered it can be an excellent, speedy and thorough way of recording information.

The problem-orientated approach to record keeping may be used. In this system information is collated, and identified problems are analyzed and followed through. Notes can be contributed to and used by a multi-disciplinary team.

Usually referred to as POMR (problem orientated medical records), the notes are organized under four main headings:

1. Database
2. Problem list
3. Progress notes
4. Discharge summary

1. Database

All details relevant to the client are recorded on a data sheet which becomes the top sheet of the notes. Included on this sheet are personal details: name, address, date of birth, clinical details, medication and other services he is receiving.

2. Problem list

This acts as an index to the rest of the file; each problem identified as a result of assessment is numbered. Any further reference to a particular problem is prefixed by the relevant number. If the notes are to be used by other disciplines in addition to occupational therapists, there may be more than one problem list.

The following are examples of problem titles which are relevant to occupational therapists:

Person activities of daily living (PADL). Washing, dressing, grooming, feeding, continence.

Domestic activities of daily living (DADL). Ability to prepare a meal, make a drink, carry out housework, laundry and shopping.

Perception. Body image, proprioception, hemianopia, apraxia.

Sensory/motor. Specific nerve loss, sensation loss or impairment, disorder of muscle tone.

Mobility. Impaired mobility, limited mobility (indoors and outdoors), difficulty or inability to transfer from bed, chair, toilet. Mobility in bed, ability to climb stairs, ability to rise from floor following a fall, ability to use public transport.

Psychiatric state. Psychological/intellectual including memory and concentration.

Social. Relationship problems, loneliness, isolation, need for activity, outings, hobbies.

Accommodation. Access to the home and access within the home.

Work/education.

Communication.

3. Progress notes

These are written under four headings in a SOAP (subjective, objective, analysis, plan) format. However, only the relevant headings are used for each entry. Notes should be brief and only significant points should be made.

Subjective findings. These relate to personal feelings either the therapist's or the client's about problems. These must be substantive and should only be kept if essential.

Objective findings. These relate to the results of assessments. Included are recordings of range of movement and perception if relevant.

Analysis. This should reflect the therapist's professional opinion in the light of facts gained in the subjective and objective evaluation.

Plan. Short and long term aims should be listed. Each entry made in the notes should be initialled.

4. Discharge summary

The summary should be comprehensive with notes on every problem on the problem list.

REPORT WRITING

The prime purpose of writing a report is to impart information. The report should be written in a clear, concise and professional manner using terminology that will be understood by those reading it. If the report is lengthy, complex or muddled it is much less likely to be read.

If the POMR approach is used, then it may be relevant, depending on who requires the information, to copy the discharge summary instead of writing a separate report.

The following points may be helpful when writing reports:

1. Reports must be dated – this will assist in any future assessment of progress.
2. Relevant demographic data be included and clearly identifiable by the reader.
3. There should be a logical sequence of events, including an introduction and summary.
4. Any headings should be shown by the use of underlining, bold print or capital letters.
5. Spacing should be used to separate different points. A well set out report is easier to read. Itemizing using headings, points and numbers encourages clarity and helps to reduce the bulkiness of the report.
6. Abbreviations may only be used if they are clearly explained first, for example: Southern Californian Sensory Integrated Test (SCSIT), Home Visit (HV), raised toilet seat (RTS).
7. Ambiguous statements should be avoided and reports should be objective rather than subjective in observations and statements. Statements and observations should also be qualified. For example, the statement 'Mrs Smith was unwell when visited' could be written as: (a) 'Mrs Smith stated she was unwell when visited', or (b) 'Mrs Smith appeared unwell when visited, her complexion was pale and her verbal pauses were not spontaneous, which is unusual for her'.
8. It is important to use terminology which will be understood by the reader. For example, describing a client as suffering from anxiety neurosis may be interpreted by a person with little knowledge of psychiatric terminology as anxiety and neurotic. The meaning in this case has been changed completely.
9. The report should be grammatically correct. The writer must be consistent avoiding changing tense, e.g. from past to present, changing from third to first person. She should also check that spellings are correct.
10. Reports should be typed wherever possible. If they are hand-written they should be easily legible.

11. If diagrams are included they should be clearly labelled.
12. The writer should sign all reports and include her professional status.

Data Protection Act

Many departments use computers to store information rather than keep handwritten records. If this is the case, knowledge of the Data Protection Act is essential and staff must be made fully aware of their personal liability for confidentiality.

The Data Protection Act became law on 12 July 1984. It is the first piece of legislation in the United Kingdom concerned with the use of computers. Its purpose is to protect information about individuals and to enforce a set of standards for the processing of such information.

The provisions of the Act are being brought into force piecemeal.

From May 1986 it became illegal to hold or process personal data unless the user was registered in doing so. As a result of the Act, a Data Protection Registrar was appointed to hold a public register of computer systems. Usually it is the employing authority which registers as the data user. Decisions as to the contents and use of data are in most instances made by individual employees who are exercising control on behalf of their employer. Data users must register the following information:

- The personal data they hold
- The purposes for which they use personal data
- The sources from which they collect such data
- Those to whom they disclose such data
- The countries to which a transfer of such data may occur

By 1987 the Act gave individuals a right to know what is held about them on computer, to correct it if it is wrong and to erase it if irrelevant. An individual has a right to claim financial compensation if the courts decide that any damage or distress has been caused as a result of unauthorized disclosure or inaccuracy of personal data. The Secretary of State however may exempt access to personal data on the grounds that an individual's well-being could be damaged if he were to be given personal health information.

The public register is the means by which an individual will be able to gain access to personal data. He can make a request in writing to the data user for a copy of his personal data. The user then has up to 40 days to supply the necessary information. An adequate check must be made on the identity of the person requesting this information.

A number of definitions are carried by the Act:

Data. This is information recorded in a form which can be processed by equipment.

Data users. These are organizations or users who control the contents and use of a collection of personal data.

Data subject. This is an individual about whom information is held.

Personal data. This is information about a living individual, and includes expressions of opinion about him but does not include any indication of the intentions of the data user in respect of that individual.

Computer Bureaux. This is an individual or organization who processes data for other data users or who allow other data users to process personal data on their equipment.

REFERENCES AND FURTHER READING

Brechin, A. and Liddiard, P. (1981) *Look at it This Way – New Perspectives in Rehabilitation.* Hodder and Stoughton in association with The Open University Press.
Data Protection Act (1984) HMSO, London.
Petrie, J.C. and McIntyre, N. (1979) *The Problem Orientated Medical Record.* Churchill Livingstone.
Schell, P. and Campbell, A. (1972) POMR – not just another way to chart. *Nursing Outlook,* **20**, 510–14.

11

Benefits and allowances

The Department of Social Security (DSS) has made some attempt in recent years to publicize the range of financial benefits available to the general public. Information leaflets are now written in plain English, a style which is easier to understand and in a larger, bolder typeface. In spite of this effort, thousands of pounds remain unclaimed each year. This is partly due to a general lack of information and knowledge about the range of services and benefits available.

Information leaflets are obtainable from post offices and DSS offices, but if a disabled or elderly person is housebound, or his local office is inaccessible, he may have difficulty first, in finding or obtaining relevant leaflets and secondly discussing his financial situation with a DSS officer.

Other reasons for not taking up benefits may include the difficulty in completing application forms or they may be reluctant to claim what they see as charity.

Therapists, too, are often unaware of the range of benefits available. They may believe it is not their responsibility to be concerned with matters other than functional assessments. However, all professionals have a responsibility for advising people on benefits and allowances available. It is often sufficient to be familiar with the scope of benefits available rather than have an in-depth knowledge of each one. Therapists need to know how to apply for benefits and how to appeal if a claim is turned down.

Therapists should advise their clients to complete application forms with as much detail as possible and not assume that DSS officers will already know in detail about their particular circumstances. If a person is in doubt about his entitlement to a particular benefit, he should always claim. It is possible to arrange for a DSS officer or other official responsible for administering benefits to visit a disabled person in his home if he needs further advice. Citizens' Advice Bureaux and Law Centres should also offer advice as will social workers.

In April 1988 major changes to Social Security benefits were introduced by the government. Three main benefits were changed: family income supplement (FIS) was replaced by family credit, the rules for housing benefit were changed, and supplementary benefit was replaced by income support. There are currently a great many debates about the amount of money people lose under new scheme. Whether the new system is less complicated than its predecessor, as claimed by the government, is open to question. In order to enable people to receive the maximum amount, occupational therapists must make every effort to obtain clear and accurate information, or at least refer disabled people to relevant organizations for assistance.

Full details of benefits available, criteria for eligibility, how to claim, how claims are decided and how to appeal against unsuccessful claims are given in relevant social security factsheets and leaflets. Details are given at the end of this chapter. The following is a brief summary of some of these benefits.

Attendance allowance

This is a tax-free cash allowance which is non-means tested and does not depend on having paid National Insurance contributions. It is non-taxable. Its aim is to provide financial assistance to people, who because they are sick or disabled, mentally or physically, require help from another person, either continually, or during the day or by night. The allowance is paid to the person claiming it and not the carer. It is payable even to someone living alone. A carer does not need to be named in the application.

Attendance allowance is not paid to those living in hospital or local authority residential home, boarding schools, colleges or training centres, or any other place which is provided or helped by public money. Payment does however continue if a person normally lives at home but is admitted to a hospital or residential home for a short period of respite care.

The Family Fund

This is a lump-sum grant. The grant is not means tested, but a family's economic and social circumstances are taken into account. The Family Fund is financed by the government, but administered by the Joseph Rowntree Memorial Trust. Its aim is to provide funds to cover the cost of specific items required by families caring for severely physically or mentally handicapped children under 16 years of age. For example, payment for the hire of cars or to pay taxi fares for specific outings, payment for a washing machine in the case of a child who is incontinent, payment for clothing, bedding or furniture, payment for holidays or payment towards removal expenses. The fund complements existing help which is available through statutory and voluntary organizations. Claims however cannot be made towards the cost of private medical treatment, private education, to offset debts incurred as a result of the needs of the child or to provide any services which should be the responsibility of the local authority or statutory bodies. Furthermore, if a child is cared for by foster parents or is in the care of the local authority then the fund cannot be paid.

In order to apply to the fund, a specific application form must be completed. This is available from The Family Fund, PO Box 50, York YO1 1UY.

Family Credit

Family Credit is a tax-free social security benefit which replaced family income supplement in April 1988. It is a benefit which is paid to working people who are employed or self-employed and who have at least one child. The savings of the person making the application are taken into account. People who claim family credit are not expected to pay for the following items for themselves, their partners or their children: NHS prescriptions, NHS dental treatment, travel to hospital for NHS treatment, or help with the cost of glasses.

Housing Benefit

This is a local authority administered scheme to help people with low incomes to pay for their rent and rates. Changes in housing benefit were introduced in April 1988. The benefit is payable whether or not the claimant is employed as long as he pays rent to a council or a private landlord, or if he owns his own home. He does not need to be in receipt of any other social security benefit. However, the amount of savings of the claimant are taken into account. Housing benefit can cover part, or all, of the rent and up to 80% of the rates a person has to pay in order to live in his own home. The benefit does not help with mortgage re-payments and cannot be used towards the purchase of a property. In addition it cannot be used for fuel, heating, lighting and cooking, the cost of meals that are included in rent, water charges, service charges for personal laundry and household cleaning, or rates on a business premises.

Income Support

Income Support is a social security benefit which from April 1988 replaced supplementary benefit. It aims to meet the regular weekly needs of people who do not have enough money to live on. The person applying must be either unemployed, or aged 60 years or over, or bringing up children on their own, or be too sick or disabled to work or to only work part time, or have to stay at home to look after a disabled relative. If the claimant is working, the amount earned is taken into account as is the amount of their savings. If a person is in receipt of income support then he may be entitled to other financial help such as help with rent and rates, help with a mortgage or home loan. In addition, the person will not be expected to pay for NHS prescriptions, NHS dental treatment, travel to hospital for NHS treatment or help with the cost of glasses.

Industrial Injuries and Diseases Disablement Benefit

This is a benefit which is paid regardless of the amount of National Insurance contribution paid. It is paid in addition to sickness and invalidity benefit. The benefit is to provide financial help to people whose incapacity arises from an industrial accident or prescribed disease such as pneumoconiosis, byssinosis, occupational asthma or occupational deafness.

Invalid Care Allowance

This is a cash allowance which is non-means tested and does not depend on the claimant having paid national insurance contributions. It is however taxable. The aim of the benefit is to allow people under pension age, regardless of their marital status to remain at home in order to care for a severely disabled person. The claimant does not need to be related to the person or living at the same address. However, at least 35 hours a week must be spent in caring for the disabled person. The disabled person himself should be in receipt of the attendance allowance at either the higher or lower rate. Invalid care allowance is not paid to anyone receiving the same amount or more from one of the following benefits: maternity allowance, non-contributory invalidity pension, retirement pension, sickness or invalidity benefit, unemployability supplement, unemployment benefit, or widows benefit. If a person is in receipt of supplementary benefit, he can also claim invalid care allowance. However, if it is paid, then it will be deducted from the supplementary benefit.

Invalidity Benefit

Invalidity Benefit is non-taxable. The payment of the benefit depends on the claimant's National Insurance contribution record.

Mobility Allowance

This is a cash benefit which is non-means tested and non-taxable. The benefit is to pay for the cost of outdoor mobility for people who are unable or virtually unable to walk and who are likely to remain so for at least one year. An application can be made by any person aged five years and over, but under 66 years of age. However, if the applicant applies when aged 65 years, he will have to provide evidence that he could have qualified for the allowance before he reached that age. If successful, then the allowance is paid until the claimant is 75 years.

The allowance is payable to people whether they live in their own home, in hospital or residential school or residential home. It is not discontinued if the person is admitted to hospital for any period of time. The claimant must be able to use the allowance. It will not be paid to a person who for medical reasons cannot be moved or who is in a coma. The claimant cannot claim the mobility allowance if he has either an invalid trike or car provided by the DSS under the pre-1976 vehicle scheme. It is however possible to change from this earlier scheme to receive the mobility allowance provided that the person meets the criteria laid down by the DSS for all those claiming the allowance.

Severe Disablement Allowance

This is a weekly cash benefit which is non-means tested and non-taxable. It is to provide financial help to people who have been unable to work because of long-term sickness or disablement, mental or physical, and who do not normally receive sickness or invalidity benefit because they have not paid sufficient National Insurance contributions.

The claimant must have been incapable of work continuously for 28 weeks before the first day he is paid the allowance. The incapacity must be such that it satisfies the DSS 80% disablement rules.

A person will be treated as 80% disabled if:

1. he receives the attendance allowance;
2. he receives mobility allowance;
3. he receives the war pensioners' mobility supplement;
4. he is registered by a local authority as blind or partially sighted or is profoundly deaf;
5. he has already been found to be 80% disabled for industrial injuries disablement benefit or for a war disablement pension;
6. he has received a vaccine damage payment;
7. he has an invalid trike or an invalid car or a private car allowance from the DSS.

If none of these applies, then a doctor will decide whether a person is 80% disabled as specified by the DSS.

The Social Fund

The Social Fund was introduced in April 1988. It is a scheme to help those with exceptional expenses which are difficult to pay from their regular income. Three payments are available: budgeting loans, crisis loans and community care grants. Only a limited amount of money is available for these payments, which are made at the discretion of social fund officers.

Statutory Sick Pay

Statutory Sick Pay is paid weekly and depends on average weekly earnings rather than National Insurance contributions. The benefit is to provide money to a person who is incapable of work due to sickness for the first 28 weeks of their sickness. Employers are responsible for paying this sum to employees. At the end of 28 weeks, statutory sick pay is usually replaced by Invalidity Benefit.

REFERENCES AND FURTHER READING

Avery, L. (1983) *Disability: Counting the Costs*. Disability Alliance Educational and Research Association.
Disability Rights Handbook. Published annually with quarterly update. Disability Alliance Education and Research Association.

Social Security factsheets and leaflets:
RR1 *Help with Housing Costs*
RR2 *A Guide to Housing Benefits*
FIG5 *A Fact Sheet About Housing Benefit*
FB28 *Sick or Disabled?*
SB16 *A Guide to the Social Fund*
FIG4 *A Fact Sheet about the Social Fund*
N1261 *A Guide to Family Credit*
FIG3 *A Fact Sheet about Family Credit*
SB20 *A Guide to Income Support*
HB5 *A Guide to Non Contributory Benefits for Disabled People*
N1205 *Attendance Allowance*

12

Legislation

As with benefits and allowances, occupational therapists may feel that a knowledge of the legislation framework within which they work is unnecessary. This is not so. It is important that they are aware of Acts of Parliament which affect the services provided to elderly and disabled people. They may be used as a lever to attempt to improve services or secure assistance for disabled people.

A checklist of the principal Acts of Parliament affecting disabled people is given on pp. 177–182. The following information sets out the main provisions of some of these Acts. Acts are listed in alphabetical rather than chronological order.

Chronically Sick and Disabled Persons Act 1970

Section 1. This requires local authorities to:

1. inform themselves of the number and needs of disabled persons (as defined in Section 29 of the National Assistance Act 1948;
2. publish information on the services they provide under Section 29 of that Act;
3. ensure that any disabled person using the service is informed of any other services relevant to their needs.

Section 2. This lists services which local authorities have a duty to arrange if they consider a disabled person needs them. The level of provision made in any authority therefore depends on how it defines needs.

The services listed in the Act are:

1. Practical help in the home, such as the provision of home helps.
2. Provision or assistance in obtaining a radio, television or in using library facilities.
3. Provision of lectures, outings, games or other recreational facilities outside the home or assistance in taking advantage of educational facilities available.
4. Help in travelling to take part in these or other similar activities.
5. Assistance in obtaining housing adaptations or additional facilities in the home such as building an extension, designed to secure his safety, comfort or convenience.
6. Assistance in taking a holiday, whether provided by the local authority or not.
7. Provision of meals either in the home or at a local centre.
8. Provision of, or assistance in obtaining, a telephone and any special equipment necessary to use it.

Section 3. This requires local housing authorities to take account of the special housing needs of chronically sick and disabled persons, under Section 10 of the Housing Act 1985.

Sections 4, 5, 6 and 7. These are concerned with access. All new buildings used by the public such as shops, libraries, theatres, sports centres, civic centres must be accessible to disabled people. Emphasis is placed on providing toilets which can be used by people in wheelchairs. Where facilities are provided they must be clearly signposted.

Sections 8 and 8A. These require that similar access and facilities be provided for disabled people at places of education and employment.

Sections 17 and 18. These are concerned with making separate provision for young chronically sick or disabled people (under 65 years of age), and elderly people (over 65).

Section 21. This covers the introduction of the concessionary parking scheme for motor vehicles driven by, or used to convey disabled people (The Orange Badge Scheme).

Section 25–27. This is concerned with special education for deaf – blind children and children suffering from autism or acute dyslexia.

Chronically Sick and Disabled Persons (Northern Ireland) Act 1978.
This makes similar provision for disabled people in Northern
Ireland.

Chronically Sick and Disabled Persons (Scotland) Act 1972. This
amends Section 29 (2) of the Chronically Sick and Disabled Persons
Act 1970 so that Sections 1 and 2 apply to Scotland. References to
Section 29 of the National Assistance Act 1948 is read as Section 12
of the Social Work (Scotland) Act 1968.

Disabled Persons Act 1981

Section 1. This amends the Highways Act 1980 and the Roads
(Scotland) Act 1970. Highway authorities and local authorities are
required to:

1. have regard to the needs of disabled or blind people when placing
   lamp-posts, bollards, traffic-signs or other permanent obstructions
   in a street;
2. have regard to the needs of disabled people when considering the
   desirability of providing ramps at appropriate places between
   carriageways and footways;
3. ensure that holes in the pavement or street are properly protected.

Section 2. This amends the Road Traffic Regulations Act 1967 so
that penalties for the misuse of orange badges are increased.

Section 3. This amends the Town and Country Planning Act 1971.
Local planning authorities have a duty to draw attention to the
relevant sections of the Chronically Sick and Disabled Persons Act
1970 and the Code of Practice for Access for the Disabled to
Buildings (BS5810:1979) when giving planning permission to public
buildings, offices, shops, railways, public lavatories and educational
premises.

Section 4. This amends the Local Government (Miscellaneous Provisions) Act 1976. It draws attention to Section 6(1) and 7 of the
Chronically Sick and Disabled Persons Act and BS5810:1979 concerned with the provision of lavatories for the needs of disabled
people at places of entertainment.

Section 5. This replaces Section 7 of the Chronically Sick and Disabled Persons Act. A notice or sign indicating facilities for disabled people shall be displayed outside and inside the building. The appropriate route to the facilities shall also be displayed.

Section 6. This applies to Sections 4(1), 5(1), 6(1), 8A(1) of the Chronically Sick and Disabled Persons Act, which imposes on people undertaking the provision of public buildings certain duties as regards the needs of disabled people. Previously, provision was made 'in so far as it is in the circumstances both practicable and reasonable'. Following the 1981 Act these words were replaced by 'appropriate provision'; that is, provision in accordance with BS5810: 1979, or, in the case of educational buildings, Design Note 18. Exceptions will only be made if the developer can demonstrate that it is not practical or reasonable to make this provision.

Section 7. This is concerned with a new Section (8B) inserted in the Chronically Sick and Disabled Persons Act. The Secretary of State must report to Parliament on proposals for improving access for disabled people to public buildings and to public lavatories and those in places of entertainment, places selling food and drink and betting offices.

Disabled Persons Services, Consultation and Representation) Act 1986

This Act is sometimes referred to as the Tom Clarke Bill after its author. It comprises 18 sections which are being introduced in stages.

Sections 1 and 2. The right to representation

A disabled person now has the right to either appoint, or, in some circumstances have appointed for them a representative. The role of the representative is to assist a disabled person in putting forward his views, and ensuring that they are taken fully into account by a local authority. The Act states that a representative will only be legally recognized by a local authority when he is representing a disabled person in relation to services which are already available under existing legislation such as the Chronically Sick and Disabled Person's Act 1970.

Any person or relevant organization can be appointed as a representative. If the disabled person is under 16 years of age, then the representative is appointed by the parent or guardian. If, because of mental or physical incapacity, the disabled person is unable to appoint a representative, then the local authority can appoint the representative or authorize another organization to appoint a representative. The representative has the right to accompany the disabled person to any interview or meeting where individual needs are being discussed. In addition, the representative has the right to request any documents or information about the disabled person unless it is felt by the local authority that this would be harmful to the disabled person. If the disabled person is living in accommodation other than his own, then the representative has a right to visit him at any reasonable time, and spend time with him in private.

Section 3. The right to assessment

The Act gives three groups of disabled people the right to assessment.

Group A. Any disabled person who asks for services from the local authority listed under Section 2 of the Chronically Sick and Disabled Persons Act 1970. The local authority has an obligation to provide an assessment.

Group B. Disabled children and young people leaving full-time education. The local education authority has to inform the local authority at least eight months before the person is expected to leave full-time education provided they are under 19 years. The local authority then has to make an assessment of the individual's possible needs within five months of the notification from the local education authority.

Group C. Those who have been discharged from hospital and who have been receiving treatment continuously for six months or more for mental illness or mental handicap. As soon as a discharge date has been set then the hospital must inform the district health authority and local authority for the area the disabled person intends to live. If the person is under 19 years, then the local education authority must also be informed. The various authorities should then assess the health, welfare and educational needs of individuals.

If, following assessment, the local authority decides against providing the services requested, then a written explanation will have to be given to the disabled person or their carers. Disabled people may be asked to pay for some or all of the services which are provided to them by the local authority.

Section 9. The right to information

Local authorities are required by the Act to inform any disabled person of the range of social services provided by that authority and information about relevant services provided by other authorities and organizations.

Section 10. The right to consultation

The Act states that certain local authority committees should have a member who is disabled or who has special knowledge or experience of the needs of disabled people. The person should only be appointed after consultation with appropriate organizations of disabled people. An organization is defined as one whose policy-making body consists of at least 51% disabled people. Thus, the person chosen should represent the views of many disabled people rather than give his own personal views.

Section 8. The rights of carers

Carers have the right to ask for an assessment of the needs of the disabled person for whom they are caring for services under Section 2 of the Chronically Sick and Disabled Persons Act 1970. Carers also have the right to have their ability to continue to provide care taken into account when the needs of the disabled person are being assessed.

To be recognized as a carer, an individual must provide a substantial amount of care on a regular basis to a disabled person who is living at home. This does not apply to a person who is paid specifically to do the job.

Disabled Persons (Employment) Act 1944

Section 1. This provides a definition of 'disabled person' for the purpose of employment. Other provisions of the Act include:

- The establishment of a register of disabled people. The Disabled Persons (Employment) Act 1958 later amended the Act to allow disabled people to have their names removed from the register on written application.
- The provision of vocational training and industrial rehabilitation courses.
- The introduction of a quota scheme. Those employing 20 or more people must employ a quota (3%) of registered disabled people.
- The designation of certain categories of employment for registered disabled people.
- The provision of special facilities to enable the employment of seriously disabled people. The Disabled Persons (Employment) Act 1958 later amended this section by imposing a duty on local authorities to provide sheltered employment to registered disabled people who are resident in their areas.

Education Act 1981

This Act provides the legal framework for the assessment and placement of children with disabilities in school, either special or ordinary schools. The Act is based on the recommendations of the Warnock Committee.

Sections 1, 2, 4. The Act refers to children with any type of disability as 'children with Special Educational Needs' (SEN). A child has SEN if he has a learning difficulty which requires that special educational provisions are made for him.

Section 2. This states that all children requiring special education should be educated in ordinary schools as far as possible, and, wherever reasonably practicable, children with SEN should join in the activities of the school with other children. The views of parents and the ability of schools to meet children's special educational needs must be taken into account.

Section 5. This refers to indentification and assessment of children with SENs.

Section 6. This refers to the assessment of children under two years. Local education authorities (LEA) have a duty to assess children under two years with suspected SEN. However, the Act 'expects'

107

but does not insist that the LEA make any special provision for the child as a result of the assessment.

Housing Act 1974

Section 56. amended by Housing Rents and Subsidies Act 1975. This refers to:

1. discretionary improvement grants which may be made for the purpose of making a dwelling suitable for accommodating a disabled person;
2. mandatory intermediate grants which may be made for installing standard amenities which are lacking, or for installing suitable alternative facilities where existing amenities are inaccessible to a disabled person. Examples include lavatories, showers and baths.

Housing Act 1980

1. Increases the scope of the repairs grant so that the problem of structural disrepair in old houses can be dealt with.
2. The rateable value limit in respect of improvement grants for work required by a disabled occupant is removed.
3. Regulated tenants in private sector housing and secure tenants in public sector housing can apply for improvement, intermediate and repair grants.

Housing (Financial Provisions) (Scotland) Act 1978

Section 16. This refers to Section 1 of the Housing (Scotland) Act 1974. The definition of 'improvement' is widened to include work for a disabled occupant.

Section 3. This refers to Section 3 of the Housing (Scotland) Act 1974. The limit on the rateable value of property is removed for those applying for an improvement grant which is needed to carry out work for a disabled person.

Local Authority Social Service Act 1970

The functions of the Health and Welfare Departments and Children's Departments are combined so providing a unified service, to do this every local authority is required to set up a Social Services Committee.

Local Government and Planning (Scotland) Act 1982

This Act is concerned with improvement grants.

Section 51(a). A new provision is inserted into Section 7 of the Housing (Scotland) Act 1974 whereby improvement grants may be given for the provision of a standard amenity to meet the needs of a disabled person, regardless of the availability of any existing standard amenity.

Section 51(b). Section 5(5) of the Housing (Scotland) Act 1974 is amended. Where a grant is made for works of adaptation to meet the needs of a disabled occupant then the maximum approved expense restriction on successive grants is removed.

National Assistance Act 1948

Section 29. This seeks to define a 'disabled person'. In addition, this section empowers local authorities to promote the welfare of disabled people, including:

1. giving advice on services available;
2. giving instruction in methods of overcoming the effects of disabilities;
3. providing workshops and hostels for disabled workers;
4. providing recreational facilities;
5. maintaining a register of disabled people

Section 30. Voluntary organizations can be used and funded by local authorities to provide these services.

Sections 21 and 27. These cover the provision of residential accommodation, part III.

Social Security and Housing Benefits Act 1982

A new scheme is introduced to give help with rent and rates; Housing Benefit. Two former schemes are brought together by housing benefit; supplementary benefits payments for rent and rates and local authority rent and rate rebates and rent allowances.

Social Work (Scotland) Act 1968

Social Work Departments are to administer a unified social services.

Section 12. This provides the funding for local authorities services to clients including disabled people.

Section 14. This refers to the provision of home helps and laundry facilities.

Sections 59 and 60. This covers the provision of residential accommodations (part IV).

PRINCIPAL ACTS OF PARLIAMENT AFFECTING DISABLED PEOPLE

Access

- Building Act 1984
- Chronically Sick and Disabled Persons Act 1970
- Chronically Sick and Disabled Persons (Amendment) Act 1976
- Chronically Sick and Disabled Persons (Northern Ireland) Act 1978
- Disabled Persons Act 1981
- Local Government (Miscellaneous Provisions) (Scotland) Act 1981 Sub-sections 36 and 37

Education

- Education Act 1980 Sub-sections 8 and 9 (provision of information)
- Education Act 1981

- Education (Handicapped Children) Act 1970
- Education (Mentally Handicapped Children) (Scotland) Act 1974
- Education (Scotland) Act 1962
- Education (Scotland) Act 1981

Employment

- Disabled Persons (Employment) Acts 1944 and 1958
- Employment and Training Act 1973 Section 12
- Health and Safety at Work Act 1974

Housing

- Housing Act 1974 Sub-section 56 and 65 (improvement and intermediate grants)
- Housing Act 1980: Schedule 1 (exceptions to right to buy); Schedule 12 paragraph 7 (removal of rateable value limit for improvement grants)
- Housing and Building Control Act 1984 (Section 2 amends Schedule 1 of the 1980 Act)
- Housing (Financial Provisions) (Scotland) Act 1978
- Housing Rents and Subsidies Act 1975 Schedule 5 (minor amendments to 1974 Act)
- Land Compensation Act 1973 Section 45 (special treatment of adapted dwellings)
- Local Government Act 1972 Section 195(2) – consultation between district and county councils
- Local Government and Planning (Scotland) Act 1982
- Rates Act 1984 Schedule 1, paragraph 22 (amends the system of rate relief for institutions)
- Rating (Disabled Persons) Act 1978

Mobility

- Chronically Sick and Disabled Persons Act 1970 Sub-sections 20 and 21
- Concessionary Travel for Handicapped Persons (Scotland) Act 1980
- Disabled Persons Act 1981 Section 2 (details of penalties for

misuse of Orange Badge and for wrongful parking in reserved places)
- Road Traffic Act 1972
- Social Security (Miscellaneous Provisions) Act 1977, Section 13 (reserved rights of pre-1976 vehicle scheme beneficiaries)
- Social Security Pensions Act 1975 Section 22 (mobility allowance)
- Transport Act 1968: Section 138 (concessionary fares)
- Transport Act 1982: Section 54 (exemption for Orange Badge holders from the fitting of immobilization devices); Section 68 (refusal and withdrawal of Orange Badge and appeal rights); Section 70 (free exemption for exemption from wearing seat belts).

Social security

- Health and Social Security Act 1984: Section 11 (Severe Disablement Allowance); Section 13 (child dependency additions subject to earnings rule)
- Health and Social Services and Social Security Adjudication Act 1983 Schedule 8 (amalgamation of National Insurance and supplementary benefit adjudication)
- Security Act 1975 (principal legislation for most benefits)
- Social Security Act 1979: Section 2 (Attendance Allowance for people on dialysis); Section 3 (retention of Mobility Allowance until age 75)
- Social Security Act 1980
- Social Security Act (No. 2) Act 1980
- Social Security and Housing Benefits Act 1982 (details of sick pay and housing benefits)
- Social Security and Housing Benefits Act 1983
- Social Security Pensions Act 1975
- Pneumocomiosis etc. (Workers Compensation) Act 1979
- Vaccine Damage Payments Act 1979

Social services

- Chronically Sick and Disabled Persons Act 1970
- Chronically Sick and Disabled Persons (Northern Ireland) Act 1978

- Chronically Sick and Disabled Persons (Scotland) Act 1972
- Health and Social Security Act 1984 Sub-sections 1–4 (dispensing and fitting of optical appliances)
- Health and Social Services and Social Security Adjudication Act 1983: Section 1 (refers to joint financing); Section II (refers to registration of homes); Sub-sections 17–24 (refer to charges for local authority services)
- Health Services and Public Health Act 1968 Section 45 (refers to services for elderly people)
- Local Authority Social Services Act 1970
- National Assistance Act 1948, Part III
- National Health Service Act 1977 Schedule 2 (refers to provision of vehicles)
- Residential Homes Act 1980
- Social Work (Scotland) Act 1968

Taxation

- Finance Act 1972 Section 70 (exemption from tax of the vehicle maintenance grant)
- Finance Act 1981: Section 27 (refers to taxation of certain social security benefits); Section 30 (refers to taxation of sick pay)
- Finance Act 1982 Section 30 (exemption from tax of mobility allowance)
- Income and Corporation Taxes Act 1970 (as amended) Sub-sections 14, 16, 17, 18, 188 (1)(a), 189 (1), 219, 219A (all refer to various reliefs)
- Value Added Tax Act 1983 Schedule 5 (zero-rating): Group 4 (talking books); Group 14 (equipment for handicapped people); Group 16 (charities)

Vehicle excise duty exemption

- Finance Act 1971 Section 7 (refers to passengers)
- Finance Act 1972 Section 128 (refers to drivers)
- Finance Act 1974 Section 50 (widens the Finance Act 1971)
- Finance Act 1978 Section 8 (refers to recipients of the Mobility Allowance)
- Finance Act 1984 Section 5 (refers to recipients of War Pensioners' Mobility Supplement)

- Vehicles (Excise) Act 1971 Section 7 (refers to invalid vehicles)

Other miscellaneous acts

- Congenital Disabilities (Civil Liability) Act 1976
- Marriage Act 1983 (enables marriages of housebound people to be solemnized at home)
- Telecommunications Act 1984 Section 54 (establishes an advisory body for disabled people)
- Trading Representations (Disabled Persons) Acts 1958 and 1972

REFERENCES AND FURTHER READING

MIND/Royal Association for Disability and Rehabilitation (1988) *Disabled Persons (Services, Consultation and Representation) Act 1986. Handbook for Voluntary Organisations, Occupational Therapists' Reference Book.* Parke Sutton Publishing in association with the British Association of Occupational Therapists.

Royal Association for Disability and Rehabilitation (1984) *A Guide to the Education Act 1981.* RADAR.

13

Relevant organizations

Access Committee for England, 35 Great Smith Street, London SW1P 38J

ACTIVE, Seabrook House, Darkes Lane, Potters Bar, Hertfordshire EN6 2HL

Advisory Centre for Education (ACE), 15 Victoria Park Square, London E2 9BP

Age Concern England, Bernard Sunley House, 60 Pitcairn Road, Mitcham, Surrey CR4 3LL

Age Concern Scotland, 33 Castle Street, Edinburgh EH2 3DN

Alzheimer's Disease Society, 158–160 Balham High Road, London SW12 9BN

Arthritis Care, 6 Grosvenor Crescent, London SW1X 7ER

Association of Crossroads Care Attendant Schemes Ltd. 10 Regent Place, Rugby, Warwickshire CV21 2PN

Association for Spina Bifida and Hydrocephalus (ASBAH), 22 Upper Woburn Place, London WC1H OEP

Back Pain Association, 31–33 Park Road, Teddington, Middlesex TW11 OAB

British Database on Research into Aids for the Disabled (BARD), Handicapped Person's Research Unit, Newcastle-upon-Tyne Polytechnic, 1 Coach Lane, Coach Lane Campus, Newcastle-upon Tyne NE7 7TW

British Diabetic Association, 10 Queen Anne Street, London W1M OBD

British Limbless Ex-Service Men's Association (BLESMA), Frankland Moore House, 185–187 High Road, Chadwell Heath, Romford, Essex RM6 6NA

British Polio Fellowship, Bell Close, West End Road, Ruislip, Middlesex HA4 6LP

British Red Cross Society, 9 Grosvenor Square, London SW1X 7EJ

British Sports Association for the Disabled, 34 Osmaburgh Street, London NW1 3ND

British Telecom, 81 Newgate Street, London EC1A 7AJ

Centre on Environment for the Handicapped, 35 Great Smith Street, London SW1P 3BJ

Chest, Heart and Stroke Association, Tavistock House North, Tavistock Square, London WC1H 9JE. In Northern Ireland, 28 Bedford Street, Belfast BT2 7FE. In Scotland, 65 North Castle Street, Edinburgh EH2 3LT

Crossroads (Scotland) Care Attendant Scheme Trust, 24 George Square Glasgow G2 1EG

Cystic Fibrosis Research Trust, Alexandra House, 5 Blyth Road, Bromley, Kent BR1 3RS

Disability Alliance, 25, Denmark Street, London WC2 8NJ

Disabled Drivers' Association, Drake House, 18 Creekside, London SE8 3DZ

Disabled Living Foundation, 380–384 Harrow Road, London W9 2HU

Disablement Income Group (DIG), Mill Mead Business Centre, Millmead Road, London E1 4TR

Equipment for the Disabled, Mary Marlborough Lodge, Nuffield Orthopaedic Centre, Headington, Oxford OX3 7LD

Friedreich's Ataxia Group, Burleigh Lodge, Knowle Lane, Cranleigh, Surrey GU6 8RD

Headway, National Head Injuries Association, 200 Mansfield Road, Nottingham NG1 3HX

Library Association, Medical Health and Welfare Libraries Group, 7 Ridgmont Street, London, WC1E 7AE

Loughborough University Institute for Consumer Ergonomics, 75 Swingbridge Road, Loughborough, Leics. LE11 0JB

Lupus Group, Arthritis Care, 6 Grosvenor Crescent, London SW1X 7ER

MENCAP (Royal Society for Mentally Handicapped Children and Adults), 123 Golden Lane, London EC1Y 0RT

Motor Neurone Disease Association, 38 Hazelwood Road, Northampton, NN1 1LN

Multiple Sclerosis Society of Great Britain and Northern Ireland, 25 Effie Road, London SW6 1EE

Muscular Dystrophy Group of Great Britain and Northern Ireland, Natrass House, 35 Macaulay Road, London SW4 0QP

Northern Ireland Information Service for Disabled People, 2 Annadale Avenue, Belfast BT7 3JR

Parkinson's Disease Society of the UK, 36 Portland Place, London W1N 3DG

REACH, The Association for Children with Artificial Arms, 7 Farminghen Road, Benhall, Cheltenham, Gloucestershire GL51 6AG

Rehabilitation Engineering Movement Advisory Panel (REMAP), 25 Mortimer Street, London W1N 8AB

Royal Association for Disability and Rehabilitation (RADAR), 25 Mortimer Street, London W1N 8AB

Royal National Institute for the Blind, 224 Great Portland Street, London W1N 6AA

Royal National Institute for the Deaf, 105 Gower Street, London WC1E 6AH

Scottish Council on Disability, 5 Shandwick Place, Edinburgh EH2 4RG

SKILL, National Bureau for Students with Disability, 336 Brixton Road, London SW9 7AA

Spastics Society, 12 Park Crescent, London W1N 4EQ

Spinal Injuries Association, Yeoman House, 76 St. James' Lane, London N10 3DF

SPOD (Association to Aid the Sexual and Personal Relationships of the Disabled), 286 Camden Road, London N7 0BJ

Talking Book Service for the Blind, Mount Pleasant, Wembley, Middlesex HA0 1RR

Welsh Council for the Disabled, Caerbragdy Industrial Estate, Bedwas Road, Caerphilly, Mid-Glamorgan CF8 3SL

Index